SUFFERING FROM THE CHURCH

SUFFERING FROM THE CHURCH

Renewal *or* Restoration?

Heinrich Fries

Arlene Anderson Swidler
and Leonard Swidler
Translators

Forewords
Leonard Swidler
Peter Neuner

A Liturgical Press Book

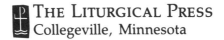
THE LITURGICAL PRESS
Collegeville, Minnesota

This book was originally published, other than the forewords, in German under the title *Leiden an der Kirche*, © 1989 Verlag Herder Freiburg im Breisgau.

Cover design by Greg Becker

1   2   3   4   5   6   7   8   9

Library of Congress Cataloging-in-Publication Data

Fries, Heinrich.
    [Leiden an der Kirche. English]
    Suffering from the church : renewal or restoration? /
Heinrich Fries ; Arlene Anderson Swidler and Leonard Swidler, translators ; forewords, Leonard Swidler, Peter Neuner.
    p.   cm.
    Includes bibliographical references.
    ISBN 0-8146-2172-4
    1. Church renewal—Catholic Church. 2. Catholic Church—History—1965— I. Title.
BX1746.F7513 1994
282'.09'045—dc20
                                        94-1899
                                         CIP

Contents

Forewords

Not Resignation, But Creative Action!

Leonard Swidler

In 1989 Fr. Heinrich Fries published an essay entitled "Suffering from the Church," 150,000 extra copies of which had to be printed to meet the demand. As a consequence he quickly expanded the essay into this small book with the same title. In it he details the contrast between the Catholic Church of the Second Vatican Council and today, and all the suffering this contrast causes. The final point of the book, however, is not simply how terrible things are, but rather, a call to face the facts clearly—and then do something to improve the situation.

Father Fries' specifics naturally sometimes refer to situations in Germany—and because the Catholic Church is a universal Church, it is important that American Catholics learn about and from the Catholic Church in other lands. However, it is also important that American Catholics relate the burning issues Father Fries discusses to the American Catholic scene. To help make that connection is the purpose of these reflections.

1. Vatican Council II: A Watershed Event

Those American Catholics who were adults in the early 1960s will remember ineradicablly what a transformation the Catholic Church underwent in the 1962–65 Vatican Council II and immediately afterwards. What further made that trans-

1

formation so utterly astounding was that it was totally unexpected. To begin with, all Church authorities were caught completely off guard when in January 1959, the "interim" Pope John XXIII announced that he "had a dream"—some ten years before Martin Luther King "had a dream"—and consequently decided to convoke an ecumenical council.

The conservatives in the Church could not imagine why an ecumenical council would be ever be necessary again after the 1870 Vatican I declaration of papal infallibility: If any serious problem arose, it could be solved swiftly and efficiently by the pope's issuing an infallibly true solution; calling together all the bishops from around the world would be a messy, and expensive, affair. As later became clear, there were also other (justified) fears on the part of the conservative elements in Rome, namely, the latest version of the ancient Roman tactic of divide and conquer, *divide et impera!*

Whenever a bishop somewhere in the world entertained a new idea or tried out a new pastoral practice, he was likely to have been told by Rome that he was "odd," "stepping out of line" with his brother bishops, and therefore should cease and desist. Later, during Vatican Council II when over two thousand bishops from around the world met each other and exchanged experiences, they frequently found that they were not so "odd," that in fact there were many of them who were looking into new ideas and practices, and that it was often the Vatican *curia* that was "stepping out of line" with the brother bishops by quashing their endeavors.

However, it would be a mistake to think that the great majority of bishops then were really closet liberals who immediately began to put into action their transforming ideas as soon as they arrived in Rome for the beginning of the Council in September, 1962. The contents of the eight huge volumes of the Council-preparatory responses and recommendations resulting from the *curia's* inquiries addressed to all the bishops around the world would clearly lead to an expectation of "more of the same."

Probably this was partly due to the bishops' internalizing the directives from Rome over the years, but it even more so underlines the stark fact that the encounter of the bishops with each other, and *most* importantly, with the critical-thinking, progressive theologians who were brought to the Council as theological experts, *periti*. This was the catalyst for the revolutionary changes of Vatican II. These *periti* included such recently Rome-censored world-famous theologians as Karl Rahner, John Courtney Murray, Hans Küng, and Henri de Lubac. It is fundamentally their ideas, reasoning, and wording that formed the Council documents. Also immensely influential were the Protestant, Orthodox, and Jewish observers, whose advice on all the Council documents was sought—and taken very seriously.

Every fall for four years not only was the Council in session, but so also was the largest theological seminary in the history of the world, for the cadres of progressive *periti* were constantly called on to lecture on every conceivable subject that could have a bearing on the Council documents—and these lectures were regularly flocked to by hundreds upon hundreds of the bishops. Thus, the bishops of the world underwent a new four-year theological course taught by the world's best, most creative Catholic theologians. But because of the massive capabilities of the mass media, much of the Catholic world in general, as well as a large portion of the non-Catholic world, likewise participated in varying degrees in this transforming theological education.

Adult Catholics of the '60s will also remember well all of the resistance the progressive elements of the Catholic Church had to overcome in order to attain their goals. Without the irresistible force of the free, and probing, press, Vatican II would indeed have been largely "more of the same"—which is precisely what the documents were which had been prepared for rubber-stamping by the arch-conservative Cardinal Ottaviani, head of the Holy Office (previously entitled the Congregation of the Holy Inquisition) and also of the Council's Preparatory Commission.

The tried and effective tactic of secrecy was largely neutralized by the ever-present press, leading some of the conservatives at times to use less than ethical tactics, such as changing agreed-to texts while they were at the printer. The sensational, because factual and solidly documented, *Letters from Vatican*

City, written by the Redemptorist American theologian Francis Xavier Murphy under the pseudonym Xavier Rynne, details the many "dirty tricks" of the Roman conservatives before and during the first session of the Council. It reads like an international spy novel, bearing out the adage that truth can be stranger than fiction.

Despite all the efforts of the conservatives, the progressive forces that were unleashed at Vatican II were immensely successful, and the euphoric atmosphere of creative renewal, democratization, dialogue, and openness to the world continued for the first years after the Council as more and more of the liberalizing documents of the Council were implemented by a variety of documents and actions from the Vatican down to the grass-roots.

The conservative forces, however, naturally regrouped and mounted the beginning of their counter-offensive, attaining their first victory in Pope Paul VI's fateful encyclical *Humanae vitae* in 1968, condemning any use of artificial contraception—one wag referred to it as "Paul's Letter to the Fallopians." Another victory came with the "tabling" of the recommendation to change the electors of the pope from papal-appointed cardinals to delegates elected by the national bishops' conferences around the world. This decree sat on Pope Paul's desk as early as 1970, but he was dissuaded from signing it by conservative *curial* elements.

Had he made this momentous decision, the whole subsequent history of Catholic Church renewal would have been radically different. Every new pope would necessarily have had a sense of responsibility to, and more collegiality with, his "constituents," the representatives of the world Church. But most importantly, this structural change at the top would have released an irresistible movement for bishops to be elected by their "constituents," and then also for pastors to be elected in turn.

With the passing of time, progressives in the Church saw Pope Paul VI becoming increasingly hesitant and indecisive, leading many to describe him as Hamlet-like, though others remarked that during the next pontificate the progressives may well look back to Paul VI with fondness and nostalgia. Still, despite the setbacks and the growing papal hesitancy, the forward motion of Vatican II swept vigorously onward for a decade after its close in 1965 into the middle of the '70s. Heinrich Fries speaks frequently in this volume of the resounding success of the General German Synod of 1975. A similar phenomenon occurred in American Catholicism as well at about the same time: the "Call to Action" Conference sponsored by the National Conference of Catholic Bishops of the United States in 1976.

2. *The Call to Action*

As the American Catholic Church's major formal contribution to the celebration of the two-hundredth anniversary of the founding of the United States of America, the National Conference of Catholic Bishops in 1974 committed itself to the holding of a "Call to Action Conference," October 20-23, 1976, dedicated to "Liberty and Justice for All," a motto taken from the American pledge of allegiance to the flag. The project turned out to be a momentous undertaking, vastly more progressive than was expected. In that sense the Call to Action was like the Second Vatican Council, that is, when representatives of the Catholic Church came together with the power to make their own decisions corporately—in the case of the Council, the appointed bishops of the world, and in the case of the Call to Action, the appointed representatives of 152 of the 167 U.S. dioceses—the "chemical reaction" of liberalizing democracy took place.

In February 1975 Cardinal John Dearden of Detroit inaugurated the bicentennial celebration with a series of seven episcopal consultations—patterned after nationwide Congressional hearings—in various parts of the country stretched out over the next year and a half. At each a panel of bishops listened to testimony of invited experts and local persons or organizations who wished to present their views; over five hundred persons presented testimony. At the same time a program of parish discussions was held in all parts of the country, each diocese being asked to organize its own program. In addition, dioceses, parishes and Catholic organizations were asked to send in written reflections and recommendations; eight hundred thousand such "responses" from eighty dioceses, that is, about one-half the U.S. dioceses—were received. All this material, comprising seven volumes, was carefully collated and eventually shaped into eight documents (on Church, nationhood, family, personhood, neighborhood, humankind, ethnicity and race, work, multiple topics) to be submitted to the 1976 Call to Action Conference. The recommendations contained in them were at the time described as "mildly progressive."

Given who the delegates to the Call to Action Conference were, not even mildly progressive recommendations were expected to emerge from the Conference. Each diocese was invited to send nine delegates, all of whom were appointed by the local bishop; 152 dioceses (out of 167) sent a total of 1,140 delegates, including 100 bishops—half the active bishops in the U.S. There were also 92 delegates, one each from 92 national Catholic organizations, making a total of 1,340 delegates; 1,500 observers were also allowed to attend the Conference. Thus 93 percent of the delegates were bishops, or appointed by bishops, and 7 percent from national organizations. "It was not a group that expected great happenings. How mistaken the skeptics were to be!"[1]

The Conference began with a videotaped blessing by Pope Paul VI and then was quickly broken up into over two hundred small groups who were assigned to discuss specific portions of the documents drawn up ahead of time. Final texts in the small groups were eventually voted on and each emended document was submitted to the plenum, which also discussed, debated, amended (146 amendments were submitted to the plenum, 57 of which were accepted, 93 rejected, and 29 tabled for lack of time) and voted on in the final version of each document. It was a creative, stimulating exercise in parliamentary democracy.

In many ways the recommendations on the Church were the most progressive, stressing "the further development of

1. *A.D. 1977* (Hyattsville, Md.: Quixote Center, 1977) 3. It is in this 24-page tabloid publication that the texts of the Call to Action Conference and the relevant explanatory material can be found.

both structures and practices of consultation and shared responsibility at every level of the church. . . . and *fidelity to an open consultative process.*'' The Conference recommended:

> 1. That church authorities on all levels . . . hold themselves accountable to the people of God for their financial policies and practices. . . . Parish and diocesan pastoral councils should be established and share responsibilities with their pastors and bishops. . . . 2. a) That a National Review Board, composed of members of the church (bishops, clergy, religious and laity) be established to address itself aggressively to the issue of due process. . . . c) The local church must be involved in the selection of bishops and pastors.

The Call to Action did not shy away from the neuralgic sex issues, recommending ''That the National Conference of Catholic Bishops take affirmative action to respectfully petition the Holy Father . . . to allow married men to be ordained to the priesthood . . . and to allow priests to exercise the right to marry and remain in or resume the active priesthood.'' The Conference also recommended that the Church no longer ''discriminate against'' divorced and remarried Catholics, allowing them to receive the sacraments. In speaking of contraception, the Conference recommended that the American bishops ''affirm more clearly the right and responsibility of married people to form their own consciences and to discern what is morally appropriate within the context of their marriage.''

Taking a prophetic position in advance of the majority of the American Catholic people at that time, the Call to Action Conference voted to recommend that

> female children be granted the right and opportunity to serve at the altar . . . that sexist language and imagery be eliminated from all official church documents . . . that the National Conference of Catholic Bishops . . . promote the full participation of women in the life and ministry of the church . . . to assure the equal status of women, a. by effecting their participation in decision making and leadership at all levels of church institutions . . . b. by guaranteeing women equal access to professional theological and pastoral training in seminaries . . . initiate

dialogue with Rome . . . to allow women to be ordained to the diaconate and priesthood.

Perhaps even more prophetic were the recommendations concerning homosexuality, including "that the church actively seek to serve the pastoral needs of those persons with a homosexual orientation, to root out those structures and attitudes which discriminate against homosexuals as persons and to join with the struggle by homosexual men and women for their basic constitutional rights" (a position far in advance of the Vatican's 1992 missive to bishops urging them precisely to discriminate against homosexuals in certain areas of life, e.g., the military, education).

All the recommendations concerning internal Church matters were in a way summed up in the extended recommendation "that the bishops of the United States, in consultation with canon lawyers, theologians and other scholars, and in cooperation with representatives of the entire church, prepare a bill of rights for Catholics in the United States," with basic specifics provided.

Bearing in mind that these recommendations, and many more, were debated and passed—at the end of a two-year nationwide intense inquiry—by bishops and bishop-appointees from almost all the dioceses of the U.S., Cardinal Dearden reported on November 1, 1976 to all the American bishops meeting at the semiannual gathering of the National Conference of Catholic Bishops that "in general the actions recommended to us indicate a realism, an independence, and a critical and mature judgment remarkable in a first assembly conducted along democratic lines . . . our response should make clear our continuing commitment to co-responsibility." Unfortunately, as in Germany and its 1975 General Synod, the end of the first decade after the end of Vatican II also marked the high point of the Council's renewal and reform thrust. After then the forces of restoration increasingly gained the upper hand. Efforts to implement the recommendations of the Call to Action were largely frustrated, partly by the conservative forces in the U.S., but mostly by the increasingly repressive actions stemming from Rome. Clear examples of the latter can be seen in the series of repressive actions taken during this period against many of the most famous theologians of Vatican II, such as, Hans Küng, Edward Schillebeeckx, and Bernard Häring. The latter, for example, was mercilessly harassed—even though he was deathly ill with cancer—by the Vatican Holy Office between 1975 and 1979.[2] Then came Pope Paul VI's death in 1978 and his replacement first by the briefly reigning John Paul I and then the long-reigning John Paul II, beginning late in 1978.

3. Pope John Paul II and Restorationism

1979 was a bad year. It had started bad—and was ending worse. At 3:00 A.M. on December 18, the phone rang insistently in the Swidler household, and when it was eventually answered, groggily, an American theologian in Rome, Edward Grace, said breathlessly: ''The Vatican just condemned Hans Küng!'' Obviously shortly after John Paul II took power the headhunters at the Holy Office had been quickly unleashed, for the following sequence of events occurred:

1) As early as the spring of 1979 the French Dominican theologian Jacques Pohier had been silenced for his book *When I Speak of God*;
2) in July the book on sexuality by a team of four American theologians was condemned;
3) in September the Jesuit General in Rome Fr. Pedro Arrupe was forced to send a letter to all Jesuits warning them that they could not publicly dissent from any papal position;
4) all fall accusations of heresy against Edward Schillebeeckx were recurrently issued in drum-beat fashion; December 13–15, Schillebeeckx was ''interrogated'' by the Holy Office in Rome;
5) that same month writings of Brazilian liberation theologian Leonardo Boff were ''condemned'' (he was later silenced);
6) then on December 18—at exactly the same time Pope John Paul II said, ''Truth is the power of peace. . . . What should one say of the practice of combating or silencing those who

2. See Bernard Häring, *My Witness for the Church*, Introduction and translation by Leonard Swidler (New York: Paulist Press, 1992), especially 90–188.

do not share the same views?''[3]—the Holy Office issued a
Declaration on Hans Küng saying he "can no longer be considered a Catholic theologian."

A few hours later Leonard Swidler was on the phone with
Fr. Charles Curran of The Catholic University of America and
Fr. David Tracy of the University of Chicago—the former one
of the foremost American Catholic moral theologians (and later
given the same inquisitorial treatment as Küng), and the latter
clearly the most creative American Catholic fundamental theologian.

We moved quickly to issue a press statement by U.S. Catholic theologians stating that "Küng was indeed a Catholic theologian." We decided to fight Rome with earlier Roman tactics,
and took a leaf from Caesar: *America est omnis divisa in partes
tres.* For the next twenty-four hours each of us got on the phone
to our third of America. As we spoke with people, time and
again the refrain recurred: This can't go on! Who will be next?
We cannot allow Rome simply to continue to *Divide et impera!*
We have got to organize!

4. The Founding of the Association for the Rights of Catholics in the Church (ARCC)

In the next days Leonard Swidler drew up a proposal to
organize what became ARCC and sent it around to all interested
contacts. The response was overwhelmingly positive, and on
March 7–9, 1980, the Founding Convention of ARCC was held
in Milwaukee, with thirty delegates from nine cities, with or-
ganizing groups from another eight cities indicating support
without sending a delegate.

The Association for the Rights of Catholics in the Church
(ARCC), was thus founded in 1980 "to institutionalize a collegial
understanding of Church in which decision-making is shared
and accountability is realized among Catholics of every kind
and condition. It affirms that there are *fundamental rights* which
are rooted in the humanity and baptism of all Catholics." It
sees its particular contribution to the Church and world in the

3. Reported in the *Washington Post*, December 19, 1979.

area of the rights of Catholics in the Church—in keeping with the urging of the 1971 International Synod of Bishops, which stated that "within the Church rights must be preserved. No one should be deprived of his ordinary rights because he is associated with the Church."

In line with the *Charter of the Rights of Catholics in the Church* issued by ARCC in 1983, after world-wide consultation,[4] and with Canon 208 of the 1983 Code of Canon Law, which states that "there exists among all the Christian faithful, in virtue of their rebirth in Christ, a true equality," and likewise with a widespread sense among the majority of the Catholic laity, ARCC rejects all divisive dualisms in Christian life, whether they take the form of dividing Church and world, men and women, clergy and laity, or others. All these pairs, springing from one source and seeking ultimately one goal, must mutually interpenetrate and cooperate. On this unity the rights of all Catholics are based: "The rights of Catholics in the Church derive both from our basic humanity as persons and from our baptism as Christians" (Preamble, *Charter*).

At the same time ARCC was being founded in the U.S., similar organizations were also launched as a result of the attack on Hans Küng in both Germany (*Christenrechte in der Kirche*) and France (*Droits et libertés dans l'Eglise*); additional reform organizations were subsequently founded—more on that below.

5. Restorationism Continues

The fifteen subsequent years of the pontificate of Pope John Paul II have been characterized by an extraordinary *Wanderlust* on the part of the pope which allowed him, among other things, to stress the honoring of human rights in the secular sphere. In this he has been indefatigable. At the same time, however, he also used his world travels as an instrument of intensive centralization of power within the Church, simultaneous with what must be described as an insistent repression of

4. The Charter is available from the ARCC office: P.O. Box 912, Delran, N.J. 08075, Tel.: 609-786-3738; it is also found with a short commentary on each of the rights in Leonard Swidler and Herbert O'Brien, *A Catholic Bill of Rights* (Kansas City: Sheed & Ward, 1989).

rights within the Church—projecting in the world a credibility-damaging image (and reality) of an ethical double-standard. There has been an alternating rhythm of severe repression, as in 1979–80, followed by a certain relenting in the face of mounting protest and resistance. All during this period Pope John Paul has been appointing conservative and ultra-conservative bishops and launching one conservative project after another, such as the recent loyalty-oath and the catechism, in moves to consolidate his centralizing, conservative power.

6. *The Maturation of American Catholicism*

However, all this Restoration activity has had less than the desired result, especially on American Catholicism, as far as the Neo-Integrists are concerned—and this is most encouraging. The profile of American Catholicism that emerged from a Gallup survey taken in the summer of 1987 just before the pope's September 1987 visit portrays a rapidly maturing Church, which maturation has continued and grown, as reflected in a summer 1992 Gallup poll.

Sunday church attendance dropped from a pre-*Humanae vitae* (1968) 65 percent to 50 percent in 1975, but has remained steady ever since (also, 87 percent of American Catholics attend church at least on some Sundays during the year).[5] Before Vatican II American Catholics were characterized by a stress on doctrinal orthodoxy, ritual regularity, and obedience to clerical authorities.[6] That docility has dramatically diminished. Now 70 percent of American Catholics surveyed think one can be a good Catholic and not necessarily go to church every Sunday. In a 1987 survey 79 percent of American Catholics opposed the Vatican prohibition on artificial birth control, and by 1992 that disagreement percentage reached 87 percent. In 1992, 74 percent of American Catholics believed

5. Andrew M. Greeley, ''Why Catholics Stay in the Church,'' *America*, 157, 3 (August 1–8, 1987) 54.

6. See Gerhard Lenski, ''The Religious Factor, 1961,'' referred to in ''NCR Gallup Poll,'' *National Catholic Reporter*, September 11, 1987, 10.

divorced and remarried Catholics should be able to remain Catholics in good standing.

In 1971, 49 percent of American Catholics were in favor of married priests; by 1983, the percentage reached 58 percent and remained stable through 1987, but by five years later the figure leaped to 70 percent.

A very clear connection between power and sex can be seen in the consistent showing that every time the Vatican publicly condemns the idea of women priests the percentage of support for it among American Catholics rises. Record-keeping started with 29 percent of American Catholics being in favor of ordaining women priests at the time of the Vatican Declaration (*Inter insigniores*) against women priests in 1977[7] to 36 percent shortly after the Vatican prohibition to 40 percent in 1979, 44 percent in 1982, 47 percent in 1985, and then a sharp jump to 60 percent in 1987 and 67 percent in 1992 (in 1992, 80 percent also favored ordaining women deacons). Perhaps even more interesting is the fact that of American Catholics under 35 in 1992, 80 percent are in favor of ordaining women priests.

By 1992, 90 percent of American Catholics said that a person could dissent from Church doctrine and remain a good Catholic, and only 26 percent thought belief in papal infallibility was necessary to be a good Catholic.

But American Catholics have not abandoned the Church in large numbers, as the drop in docility might suggest would happen. Rather, they are staying in.[8] As sociologist Teresa A. Sullivan says, ''There is something American Catholics find in Catholicism that is deep and nurturing and doesn't have very much to do with the Vatican and the bishops and all the rest.''[9] At the same time, sociologist Ruth A. Wallace notes that the Gallup survey finds among American Catholics an ''eager-

7. Cf. Leonard Swidler, ''Roma Locuta, Causa Finita?'' in: Leonard and Arlene Swidler, ed., *Women Priests: A Catholic Commentary on the Vatican Declaration* (New York: Paulist, 1977) 3.

8. Greeley, ''Why Catholics Stay in the Church'': ''In 1960, the proportion of those who were raised Catholic but no longer defined themselves as Catholic was 12 percent. In 1985 . . . that rate had risen to 13 percent'' (54).

9. ''NCR Gallup Poll,'' 10.

ness with which the laity seem to want to participate in a lot of policy questions, no matter what age or level of education."[10] The 1987, and still more the 1992, survey further strengthen what Joseph Fichter, S.J. found in 1977:

> The church is being modernized in spite of itself. It appears that the changes are occurring at the bottom of the structure. American Catholicism is experiencing adaptation at the grass roots. The most significant aspect of this change is the switch of emphasis in the basis of moral and religious guidance. Dependence on legislation from above has largely switched to dependence on the conscience of the people.[11]

Even more interesting in both Gallup survey figures are those reflecting the attitudes of the large bulge in the American population, the so-called "baby-boomers," those born between 1948 and 1957. They represent not only a disproportionately large segment of the American population, but because the Catholic "baby-boom" was even larger than in America in general, they are really the trend-setters for the future of the American Catholic Church. And they are much more liberal than the average, much more pro-democracy, pro-reform in the Church. The same is also true of educated Catholics: the more educated the Catholics, the greater the likelihood of their being liberal, pro-renewal and reform, more mature—and American Catholics are rapidly becoming increasingly more educated.

Part of this process of "maturation" of American Catholicism is the fact that even though the 1976 Call to Action was not seriously implemented and that it is over a dozen years since ARCC was founded (1980), instead of simply fading away ARCC continues to strengthen, the Call to Action has taken national organizational form, and a number of other progressive Catholic organizations have been founded since John Paul II ascended the papal throne in 1978. Then in 1991, over a dozen of these organizations banded together in a mutually supportive federation, Catholic Organizations for Renewal (COR). In

10. Ibid.
11. Joseph H. Fichter, "Restructuring Catholicism: Symposium on Thomas O'Dea," *Sociological Analysis*, 38 (1977) 163f.

addition, ARCC has for years had liaisons in Germany, France, Poland, Central America, South America and Australia, and in 1992 affiliated with the European Conference For Human Rights In The Church: A Federation Of Catholics In: Austria, Belgium, Great Britain, France, Germany, Ireland, Italy, Netherlands, Switzerland.

7. A Call for a Catholic Constitutional Convention

Most recently an idea whose time has come has surfaced, namely, the calling of a Catholic Constitutional Convention, The countries of Eastern Europe, which most of us feared would not experience democracy in our lifetime, have burst through to freedom and have either drastically restructured their constitutions, or, like Poland, the pope's homeland, formed them anew. Those who downgraded the human rights of freedom and democracy to secondary or tertiary human values have learned that the vast majority of humankind places them at the primary level.

Catholics are no less human than the citizens of Poland, Hungary, Czechoslovakia, and the other recently freed countries in the valuing of and demand for human rights and democracy—within the Church. The time is right for Catholics also to work toward the calling of a Catholic Constitutional Convention!

Such an international convention to decide on the fundamental constitutive structures of the Catholic Church which would include laity and clergy, of course, is not a radical, new departure from tradition. Very much to the contrary. It is a return to the founding tradition, to the traditions of the first "constitutional conventions"—in the language of the then dominant political reality, the Greek-speaking Roman Empire "Ecumenical Councils." Those formative Ecumenical Councils not only had lay as well as clerical participants, but were even called by the laity, the Emperor—one of them a woman!—and were not accepted as official until they were promulgated by the Emperor.

It is time, then, for all Catholic organizations and individuals to begin to plan for the third millennium's Ecumenical

Council—in the language of the now dominant political reality, democracy: a Catholic Constitutional Convention. The tone of the whole project would be totally positive. For example, the beginning of the call for the Convention might read:

> As the civil world at large is dramatically moving toward democracy, framing anew the fundamental principles of humanity, which is "created in the image of God," in constitutions, so too is the Catholic Church. . . . Following the inspiration of Vatican II and Popes John XXIII, Paul VI and John Paul II in their vigorous advocacy throughout the world of Human Rights, we committed Catholics are issuing a call to a "Catholic Constitutional Convention". . . .

As a step in that direction the following reflections, grouped in two clusters, are offered as an initial stimulus for all to think creatively and discuss widely.[12] The recommendations of the 1976 Call to Action, the ARCC *Charter of the Rights of Catholics in the Church,* along with the fundamental rights imbedded in the 1983 Code of Canon Law, would be obvious sources for the resultant Constitution of the Catholic Church.

A. Structures for Decision-making and Due Process

Mindful of the 1971 Bishops' Synod's statement that "the members of the Church should have some share in the drawing up of decisions . . . for instance, with regard to the setting up of *councils at all levels,*" the Call to Action and the ARCC *Charter* claim that "all Catholics have the right to a voice in decisions that affect them" (*Charter,* Right 5), "the right to be dealt with fairly" (Charter, Right 9), and "the right to timely redress of grievances" (Charter, Right 10).

Whatever structures for the governance of the Church are arrived at, they should include these principles:

> a) Election of leaders, including pastors, bishops and pope, through an appropriate structure giving serious voice to all respective "constituents."

12. Ideas and recommendations can be sent to the ARCC Charter Committee (7501 Woodcrest Ave., Philadelphia, Pa., Tel.: 215-477-1080; FAX: 215-477-5928; E-mail: DIALOGUE@VM.TEMPLE.EDU).

b) A limited term of office for such leaders, as has been the case for centuries in religious orders.[13]

c) A separation of powers, along with a system of checks and balances, including parish, diocesan, national and international councils, and a separate judicial system, to share the responsibility in appropriate ways with pastors, bishops and pope.

d) Establishment of the principle of dialogue to arrive at the most helpful formulations and applications of the teachings of the tradition from the local through to the highest universal level.

e) Equitable representation of all elements of the faithful, including women and minorities, in all positions of leadership and decision-making.

Structures that could support many of these rights already exist, but they are inadequately developed and, for millions of Catholics, they do not exist in actuality.[14]

Therefore, in line with the Call to Action and the ARCC *Charter*, the following steps should be taken now:

I. That in every parish and diocese
    a) pastoral councils be made mandatory,
    b) that these councils be representatively elected,
    c) that they have real decision-making power so that responsibility for the welfare of the community and its mission will be truly shared among clergy, religious and laity.

II. That every diocese have courts to redress grievances of all types according to due process (following the recommendations of the Canon Law Society of America); this might be handled by

13. See Leonard Swidler and Arlene Swidler, eds., *Bishops and People* (Philadelphia: Westminster Press, 1970) for the historical, scriptural, canonical, and theological foundation for the election of Church leaders and their limited term of office.

14. See the excellent introductory essay on the realization of rights already existing in the new 1983 Code of Canon Law by Professor James Coriden in Leonard Swidler and Patrick Connor, eds., *A Catholic Bill of Rights* (Kansas City: Sheed & Ward, 1988); *"Alle Katholiken haben das Recht . . ." Freiheitsrechte in der Kirche* (Munich: Kösel Verlag, 1990).

a) extending the scope of existing marriage tribunals, as contemplated by the 1983 Code, or by
b) new administrative tribunals, also allowed by the Code. In any case, a truly just and effective system must be made mandatory, widely promulgated and implemented.

III. That there be set up on both the national and international levels representatively elected synods of clergy and laity with real decision-making responsibility along with the national bishops conferences, Synod of Bishops, and the papacy as ongoing constitutive parts of the collegial governance of the national and universal Church.

B. The Status of Women

The most widespread and pervasive example of divisive dualism in the Catholic Church, and in society at large, is that between women and men, which operates in such a way that women are discriminated against. This clearly contradicts Christian baptism, which initiates equally all, women and men, into the community of the followers of Jesus: "There is neither male nor female . . . but all are one in Christ Jesus" (Gal 3:28).

Thus, although all people have the right to define themselves, women regularly cannot exercise this right in the Church; the 1971 Synod of Bishops saw this when it felt the need to state: "We also urge that women should have their own share of responsibility and participation in the community life of society and likewise of the Church." Unfortunately that recommendation has not yet been effectively implemented; until it is and until sufficient and adequate role models of women in leadership in the Church are provided, many women will not be able, or willing, to join actively in the Church life.

Therefore, in line with the Call to Action and the ARCC *Charter*, the following steps should be taken now:

IV. That every parish, diocese, national, international and other appropriate organizational units move immediately within the present possibilities of canon law to place competent women in positions of leadership and decision-making in numbers proportional to their membership: "All Catholic women have an equal right with men to the

resources and the exercise of all the powers of the Church''
(*Charter*, Right 26).

V. That every parish, diocese, national, international, and
other appropriate organizational unit move immediately
to appoint competent women in all liturgical offices within
the present possibilities of canon law in numbers proportional to their membership. This includes readers, com-
mentators, cantors, leaders of prayers, ministers of baptism
and Communion, and Mass servers.[15]

VI. That laity, priests and bishops through every appropriate
agency urge the Vatican to move to bring competent
women as quickly as possible into the diaconate, presbyter-
ate and episcopacy: ''All Catholics, regardless of . . . sex
. . . have the right to exercise all ministries in the Church
for which they are adequately prepared, according to the
needs and with the approval of the community'' (*Charter*,
Right 16).

VII. That every parish, diocese, national, international and
other units move immediately to eliminate all sexist and
other non-inclusive language in its documents: ''All Catholics have the right to expect that Church documents and
materials will avoid sexist language and that symbols and
imagery of God will not be exclusively masculine'' (*Charter*,
Right 32).

VIII. That every unit of the Church, and particularly the bishop,
adopt a prophetic stance in the local, regional, national,
and international communities on issues of social justice,
especially concerning what is usually the most voiceless
element of society—women.

8. Conclusion

Let this suffice as an initial stimulus for launching us on
the road to the Catholic Constitutional Convention. This convention will not occur in the immediate future, nor will the
Establishment initially move to bring it about. But thinking

15. On female Mass servers, see the respected *The Code of Canon
Law. A Text and Commentary*, commissioned by the Canon Law Society of America, Paulist Press, 1985: ''The revised Code, unlike the
1917 Code, does not prohibit females from serving Mass. . . . There
is no solid legal basis for excluding female altar servers'' (648). This
problem has at last been satisfactorily resolved by Rome.

about it, discussing and debating it and its possible content
will raise it and all it stands for—a mature, free and responsible Catholic Church—in the consciousness of Catholics
throughout the world. Then eventually it, or something like
it, will become a real possibility, and then an actualized reality.

Impossible? Who in 1958 would have thought the Vatican
II Revolution of 1962–65 was remotely possible, or the Eastern
Europe Revolution of 1989? Catholics need to have trust in God
and then work with all the creativity and energy they can mus-
ter! This is precisely the message of Fr. Heinrich Fries in this
small volume: Do not give up! Keep the faith and act so that
you, the Church and the world are better for your having lived.

Heinrich Fries: A Fundamental Theologian Assuming Ecumenical Responsibility

Peter Neuner

Heinrich Fries is one of the leading Catholic systematic theologians of the day, the Old Master of his discipline, Fundamental and Ecumenical Theology. But his name is known far
beyond that narrow world. He has always been concerned to
break through the narrow limits of purely scholarly theology
and make the results of his faith-reflections fruitful for all those
who wish to respond rationally for the faith when confronted
with the questions of our time, who can no longer be content
with merely traditional and unquestioning credulity, who have
difficulties with the Christianity served up by the Church and
for whom the Church often represents a stumbling block rather
than a help to faith.

These people, questioning, disturbed yet confident in their
faith, were and are, in addition to his theological colleagues,
the intended readership of his theology. To be understood by

them, he has written in a style that they could understand. He has proclaimed the message of the Gospel in the language of today and of our intellectual world, for only what is understood can be convincing.

The major elements of Heinrich Fries' life can be easily outlined. He was born in Mannheim in 1911 and grew up in Ödheim near Heilbronn, the oldest child in a working-class family. Because of his rather slight build, he was not suited for the profession of his father, a master blacksmith, much to his father's disappointment. He went to school, studied theology, was ordained as a priest in 1936, and in 1946, after briefly holding a position as vicar in Stuttgart and earning his doctorate and the post-doctoral Habilitation, turned to academic theology as a docent for Fundamental Theology in Tübingen. In 1950 he was promoted to professor, and in 1958 he was offered the chair of Fundamental Theology at the University in Munich, where he taught until his retirement in the autumn of 1979.

Invitations to the universities in Freiburg and Münster he declined. Cardinal Döpfner of Munich asked Heinrich Fries to accompany him to the Second Vatican Council as a Council theologian; this too he declined, as he did not wish to be given priority over his older colleagues. On the other hand, he collaborated actively in the 1971–75 General Synod of West Germany, especially in forging the document on "Pastoral Cooperation" of the Churches in the Service of Christian Unity."

The duties of a professor include both teaching and research. Fries' bibliography lists more than fifty books and almost twelve hundred articles. The book publications embrace the entire scope of fundamental theology as Fries broadly interprets it. His first love was the English religious philosopher and theologian John Henry Newman, on whom he wrote his doctoral dissertation in 1942. In 1949 he published his Habilitation volumes *Contemporary Catholic Philosophy of Religion* [the titles here are translated into English; the original titles, plus any published English translations, are given in a select bibliography at the end]. Max Scheler was the center of this research. Fries carried this philosophical dialogue further, notably with Karl Jaspers and his conception of revelation and faith, in *Is Faith a Betrayal of Humans?* (1950). Discussion of the correct understanding of and the laying of a foundation for faith resulted in his *To Believe—To Know* (1960), *What Does It Mean to Believe?* (1969), *Faith and Church Under Examination* (1970), *Faith and Church as Offering* (1976), *An Understanding Faith* (1978), *Faith and Church at the End of the Twentieth Century* (1979), *Service to the Faith* (1981). In the course of this discussion, the problematic of the critique of religion, of discussion with atheism, was added, finding its most probing expression in *Departure from God?* (1968, most recent revision in 1991), *I See No God* (1971) and *God, the Question of Our Time* (1973).

A second focus of Heinrich Fries' work was and is the teaching on the Church. The leitmotif, seen already in the title of the first book dedicated to this problem area, is one which flows through all his ecclesiological works like a *cantus firmus, The Church as an Advocate for Humanity* (1954). What was here addressed programmatically was then further elaborated in his *Church as Event* (1958), *Aspects of the Church* (1966), *Irritation and Contradiction* (1965) as well as in "Changes in the Image of the Church" in the multi-authored volume *Magisterium Salutis* (1972). In view of tendencies in today's Church he has also allowed himself an increasingly critical tone in the past few years: from a much-discussed and widely-circulated lecture came this book, *Suffering from the Church* (1989), and on his eightieth birthday on December 31, 1991, he published his reflections on his experiences with the Church under the title *There Remains Hope* (1991). After some hesitation he also wrote an essay for the book *The Angry Old Men in the Church,* but it was an "anger out of love," as he put it, which drew him to write.

In his large *Fundamental Theology* (1985) Heinrich Fries produced a synopsis of his life's work, which summarized the fruit of his teaching and research. This book is significant for Fries' theology in the same way *Foundations of Christian Faith* (1978) is for Karl Rahner's: it is and remains an accurate starting point into the fullness of his thought. Here, sketched in a compressed form, are the conclusions of his theology and his goals. The fundamental theology of Heinrich Fries is characterized by a consistent anthropocentrism: each of its individual themes proceeds from human reality and human experience, hopes and desires. It investigates the human orientation toward the transcendence that one expects and longs for without being able to achieve by oneself. And Fries describes how this ultimate desire is taken up and brought to its fulfillment in the event of revelation. Human yearning and divine revelation stand for him in one indissoluble correlation in which the answer actually corrects the human question. Faith thus appears not as a burden which must be borne obediently because of divine authority but rather as the fulfillment of humans, their hopes and desires.

Karl Rahner once caricatured the traditional relationship of fundamental theology and dogmatics in this way: Revelation comes like a closed sack. Fundamental theology has the task of testing whether the identity of the shipper is certain and whether the sack has the proper seal. Then the sack is handed on to the dogmatic theologian, who opens it and investigates the contents, which, thanks to the work of the fundamental theologians, he knows comes from God. Heinrich Fries uses a different methodology. In order to remain *au courant*, he opened the sack as a fundamental theologian and then examined the contents as well. He wants to show their significance for human questions and hopes. His fundamental theology assumes faith on the basis of Christian conviction and determines whether it is legitimate and capable of standing fast before the forum of reason and scholarship.

Thus this approach, different from that of more conventional fundamental theology not only in form but more especially in content, produces an account of faith and the basis of Christian *hope*: it demonstrates their significance for a happy and fulfilled human life. Heinrich Fries summarized the program of his fundamental theology as, "Human nature is a cry for the supernatural." Only if God enters the picture as the opposite of ambiguity, as the fulfillment of all longing, can humans be happy. There can be no correct image of humans without God, for to speak of the human is to speak of God, as Heinrich Fries repeats again and again in concert with Jaspers and Bultmann.

For a broader readership the name of Heinrich Fries is linked with the area of ecumenism. He was drawn into this by his work on Newman. His attempts at dialogue with representative Protestant theology of the twentieth century can be seen in his *Bultmann-Barth and Catholic Theology* (1955), *Response to Asmussen* (1958), and *The Contribution of Theology to the Una Sancta* (1961). Since the Council the ecumenical problematic has more and more become the center of his scholarly work. During this time the Ecumenical Institute was established at the University in Munich, and soon thereafter a Protestant Theology Department was formed where Fries found in Professor Wolfhart Pannenberg a most ideal conversation partner both for scholarly discussion and for a continuing education of students in ecumenical questions. Here ideas were raised that continue to have influence and even today are still fruitful in a variety of ways. This resulted in further publications, e.g., *One Faith—One Baptism—Separated by Eucharist* (1971), *An Ökumene Instead of Confessions* (1977).

The theses produced by Heinrich Fries and Karl Rahner together as a basis for discussion formed the highpoint and synopsis of his labors: *Union of the Churches—A Real Possibility* (1983). The book advocated the idea that the Churches today could with good will put forward the presuppositions which would make the unification of Christianity possible. In such a union today's Churches would not simply cease to exist, subordinate themselves to what might be a centrally-ruled Roman Church, or take on a uniform shape. Rather the Churches ought to end their mutual rejection, acknowledge one another, and in this way fructify and enrich one another. Fries advocates the model of conciliatory diversity, according to which differences are not boundaries but rather conditions of unity and unification. Such unification is possible if the Churches stand together on the ground of Holy Scripture and the early Christian confessions of faith. With regard to later doctrinal developments, on the other hand, broad differences are legitimate; they do not disrupt unity if the Churches do not as a result reject one another's final binding decisions to actualize the Christian message. But Churches need not themselves accept what other Churches have over time developed in their own special traditions. This degree of unity, which has already been achieved today or could be achieved on the basis of theological advances is, he is convinced, adequate for a mutual recognition of ecclesiastical offices and thus also for an acceptance of Eucharistic hospitality. Heinrich Fries is convinced that it is no longer the truth-question but rather only our bad Church habits which still refuse to accept Eucharistic community, at least according to the official rules of the Catholic Church.

These theses on ecumenism have also raised a dust storm among the public and led to controversies which Heinrich Fries has deliberately not avoided. He has built bridges in the ecumenical area and crossed borders into new territory. Edmund Schlink testified at a *Laudatio* at Fries' retirement in 1979 that he was a brave, a courageous man. He had brought forth his convictions even when others didn't want to hear them because they didn't follow the official line. He stood at a fork in the road and found contradictions: there are two Catholicisms—one builds bridges, the other tears them down. Heinrich Fries with his proverbial ''stubborn gentleness'' overcame the division, even when he knew that he would reap mostly contradiction and ingratitude and that his ideas would be condemned as inopportune. He never pursued theology for its own sake but rather for the sake of human beings, especially those who suffer from the divisions within Christianity and feel that in today's Churches the leaders would often rejoice more over newly-discovered (pseudo) problems and border-markings than over courageous steps toward unity.

As a bridge-builder Heinrich Fries has also been active in the intra-Catholic theological area, bringing specialists of various colors together in communal tasks. He has been the editor of *Newman Studies* and edited the series *Pathfinders and Paths* with Johann Finsterhölzl. Together with Georg Schwaiger he edited the three-volume *Catholic Theologians of Nineteenth Century Germany* and with Georg Kretschmar the two-volume *Classics of Theology*. He founded the series *Contributions to Ecumenical Theology,* and many of the articles in the *Handbook of Fundamental Theological Concepts* edited by him remain unsurpassed, though a ''new handbook'' is already available in a second edition. As a successor to Karl Rahner, Fries supervised the *Quaestiones disputatae,* perhaps the most respected theological series of its time. He was a participating co-editor of the *Internationale Ökumenische Bibliographie,* the *Ökumenische Rundschau* and *Catholica.*

Heinrich Fries has published many essays, and he has also written for newspapers and popular religious periodicals, thus helping many people in their faith and rekindling the light of faith for some. As scholar he has always remained a pastor as well. He passes on in his sermons what in his scholarly work seems important and life-giving to him. Preaching is for him a test case of theology; how could it be otherwise for someone who studied Newman! His collected sermons should be considered a part of his scholarly work. Among these are *Concerning the Partnership of God* (1975), *Concerning the Life-Giving Power of Faith* (1979), *Hope Which Heals* (1979), and *That the World May Believe* (1987).

Professors have the responsibility of pursuing their specialization in both research and teaching. As a university teacher Heinrich Fries drew many students: he supervised and led to a successful conclusion more than fifty doctoral dissertations plus six post-doctoral Habilitations. Today his former students occupy many chairs in systematic theology, not only in German-speaking lands but in the entire world: from Japan to South America and in the United States as well. Otto Hermann Pesch describes Heinrich Fries as "a great teacher." There is no Fries-school in the narrow sense of the word, for it never occurred to him to have his own personal research interests pursued by his doctoral students. But there is nevertheless a "Fries-style."

> He understands as few do how to create an atmosphere of open conversation in which his students can be themselves. Fries can wait till "the coin drops." He doesn't give his students "prescriptions." He enters with them into a communal adventure from which no one knows what will result. He critiques through objective discussion, not through making corrections. Thus he does not provoke "patricide" in the pursuit of self-discovery. This openness is the result, indeed a part, of his theology.[1]

1. See Otto Hermann Pesch's remarks in *Der Anzeiger für die Seelsorge,* No. 1 (1991) 7.

I remember with gratitude the seminar sessions in which I as a beginner and backbencher followed with astonishment the discussions between Johann B. Metz, Otto Hermann Pesch, Max Seckler, Johann Finsterhölzl, Jörg Splett, and Johannes Brosseder. Later, along with many others, Karl Lehmann and Leonardo Boff also appeared. Over the semester I merely listened, in some sessions hardly understanding a word, but I began to realize that I was a witness to an exciting intellectual discussion which fascinated me and drew me more and more into its spell.

It is as a consequence of this theology that Heinrich Fries takes his readers and listeners as serious partners not only in a theoretical but also practical way, that he enters into dialogue with those around him, as it were. Such anthropocentrism makes him convincing in his encounters with others. Heinrich Fries is in his person an example of what he says and what he writes. And his listeners, his readers, his students, colleagues and co-workers gratefully recognized this in a special way: they honored him on his eightieth birthday with a formal *Festschrift*, called *In Responsibility to Faith* (1992). Thus, after *Encounter. Essays toward a Hermeneutic of Theological Conversation* (1972) and *On the Way to Reconciliation* (1982), a third *Festschrift* was dedicated to him, an honor by no means customary for German theology professors. It is a sign of the broad esteem accorded Heinrich Fries that not only such bishops as Cardinal Johannes Willebrands, Bishop Paul Werner Scheele and Bishop Walter Kasper, but also theologians who are for the most part considered the critical wing of the Church, such as Hans Küng and Johann B. Metz, contributed to this book. Heinrich Fries' ideas are taken up and developed from various points of view and in differing perspectives. The authors explain from their own point of view how theologians bear responsibility for faith and theology, for the Church and its teachings, for its relationship to the other Christian confessions and to the religions of the world.

A Select Bibliography

Listed here are the original German titles, and any published English translations, referred to in this introductory essay in the order they appear:

1. *Die katholische Religionsphilosophie der Gegenwart* (1949)
2. *Ist der Glaube ein Verrat am Menschen?* (1950)
3. *Glauben—Wissen* (1960)
4. *Herausgeforderter Glaube* (1968); English translation by William D. Seidensticker, *Faith Under Challenge* (New York: Herder and Herder, 1970)
5. *Was heist glauben?* (1969)
6. *Glauben und Kirche auf dem Prüfstand* (1970)
7. *Glaube und Kirche als Angebot* (1976)
8. *Verstehender Glaube* (1978)
9. *Glaube und Kirche im ausgehenden 20. Jahrhundert* (1979)
10. *Dienst am Glauben* (1980)
11. *Abschied von Gott?* (1968, latest revision 1991)
12. *Ich sehe keinen Gott* (1971)
13. *Gott, die Frage unserer Zeit* (1973)
14. *Die Kirche als Anwalt des Menschen* (1954)
15. *Kirche als Ereignis* (1958)
16. *Aspekte der Kirche* (1963); English translation by Thomas O'Meara, *Aspects of the Church* (Baltimore: Newman Press, 1966)
17. *Ärgernis und Widerspruch* (1965)
18. "Wandel des Kirchenbildes," in: *Mysterium Salutis* (1972)
19. *Leiden an der Kirche* (1989)
20. *Es bleibt die Hoffnung* (1991)
21. "Zorn aus Liebe," in *Die zornigen alten Männer in der Kirche* (Stuttgart, 1983)
22. *Fundamentaltheologie* (1985)
23. *Bultmann—Barth und die katholische Theologie* (1955); English translation and introduction by Leonard Swidler, *Bultmann—Barth and Catholic Theology* (Pittsburgh: Duquesne University Press, 1967)
24. *Antwort an Asmussen* (1958)
25. *Der Beitrag der Theologie zur Una Sancta* (1961)
26. *Ein Glaube—eine Taufe—getrennt beim Abendmahl* (1971)
27. *Ökumene statt Konfessionen* (1977)
28. *Einigung der Kirchen—reale Möglichkeit* (with Karl Rahner, 1983); English translation, by Ruth C. L. and Eric W. Gritsch *Unity of the Churches. An Actual Possibility* (Philadelphia and New York: Fortress Press and Paulist Press, 1985)

Editorships

29. *Newman-Studien* (with Günter Biemer)
30. *Wegbereiter und Wege* (with Johann Finsterhölzl)
31. *Katholicshe Theologen Deutschlands im 19. Jahrhundert* (with Georg Schwaiger)
32. *Klassiker der Theologie* (with Georg Kretschman)
33. The book series *Beiträge zur ökumenischen Theologie*
34. *Handbuch theologischer Grundbegriffe*
35. The book series *Questiones disputatae*

Collections of Sermons

36. *Von der Partnerschaft Gottes* (1975)
37. *Von der Lebenskraft des Glaubens* (1979)
38. *Hoffnung, die den Menschen heilt* (1979)
39. *Damit die Welt glaube* (1987)

Festschriften for Heinrich Fries

40. *In Verantwortung für den Glauben* (1992)
41. *Begegnung. Beiträge zur einer Hermeneutik des theologischen Gesprächs* (1972)
42. *Auf Wegen der Versöhnung* (1982)

Introduction

The present situation in the Catholic Church, especially in West Germany, Europe, and North America, can to a large extent be described as "suffering from the Church," which differs from "suffering with the Church." The latter is inevitable when the Church, wherever it exists, comes under stress, distress, and persecution. Then there is an obligation for all Christians to unite in solidarity, for "If one part is hurt, all parts are hurt with it. If one part is given special honor, all parts enjoy it" (1 Cor 12:26).

Suffering from the Church today is not merely pain because the concrete Church lags behind its promise, its mandate, and its claims; that will always be the case. For this reason too the Church is an *ecclesia semper reformanda*, a Church which requires constant renewal but also a Church capable of such renewal. That is the basic assertion of the Second Vatican Council. We are this Church.

Suffering from the Church—an expression of a faith which believes in and loves the Church as the community of the faithful—has its concrete foundation in the fact that the Church's cohesion, its communal togetherness defined so clearly by Vatican II, has been disturbed. In other words, the present sufferings from the Church are linked to the fact that the Church today has noticeably changed from the Church of the Second Vatican Council in its authoritative judgments and mandates and is steering toward a situation which seems preconciliar, a restoration of the so-called good old days, striving to return to a time which was certainly not as good as it is often imagined to have been. And this despite the fact that words and texts from the Council are constantly being quoted by representatives of this mentality, who often choose selectively and sometimes ignore the proper context or connection.

1 The Church During the Council

During the Council, despite some controversies and unavoidable compromises as well as the exclusion of important themes and some interventions from a "higher authority," there was no suffering from the Church—apart from a few circles, then in the minority but since enormously enlarged. Rather it was a source of joy, even pride, to belong to this Church which radiated hope and confidence, which stood in solidarity with the joys and sorrows of humanity, which proclaimed the Gospel not as law but as a joyful and liberating human-friendly message, as an answer to the questions of contemporary people, especially to the question of what we humans are.

The Church of the Council sought and found a new relationship to the world as God's creation and the household of the human race. It also sought and created a new relationship to other Christian confessions, to Judaism, to the spirit of the modern age, to non-Christian religions. It argued for freedom of conscience and religion, for dialogue and cooperation as a form of encounter, and in the process it drew up principles about which, with the best of intentions, one cannot say "The Church has always. . . ." Freedom of conscience and religion had been expressly rejected in the official doctrinal statements in the past century on the principle that error has no rights. The Council on the contrary asserted that error is not a subject of justice, but people are, even if they err.

During and immediately following the Council people had no difficulty in identifying with this Church and its statements. *There was no anti-Church or anti-Rome feeling.* The Petrine office as personified in Pope John XXIII evoked universal esteem and respect and made it possible for such a papacy, with its obvious sense of brotherhood displaying the power of love, to be acceptable even outside the Catholic Church. Across the entire world the public followed the events of the Council with great approval and respect. The old Church had not been thought capable of such vitality, such encouraging youthfulness, such contagious radiance. I still remember Mario von Galli at the 1964 *Katholikentag* in Stuttgart crying out amid the tumultuous jubilation of the participants, "Church, how young you are—Church, how beautiful you are!" Today, with all the radical Church criticism which conceals nothing, no one carries on in this manner any longer.

For some Catholics today the Council has become an almost forgotten past. In addition there are today not a few voices which play down and relativize this Council—the most significant and hopeful experience in the history of the Catholic Church in our century—and the changes following it, indeed even see in it and them distorted developments which need to be revised. Instead of *Gaudium et spes,* joy and hope, today it is suppression, lamentation and listlessness which dominate the scene.

2 The Change

A change in the long, almost unbroken agreement with the official Church, its directives, and its official statements came about, in my opinion, because of Paul VI's 1968 encyclical *Humanae vitae*, which released a surge of criticism from many people, including loyal Catholics, who refused to accept so-called natural birth-control as the only morally-permitted method of birth control. Paul VI held to this decision, he said, despite the vote of the commission he himself had appointed, out of loyalty to prior Church tradition. This situation remains to this very day. On the one side there is Pope John Paul II who, with his constant emphasizing of this encyclical at every opportunity throughout the world, seems to have elevated it almost to the level of a new dogma, and on the other side there is the continuous critique of the encyclical's unconvincing argumentation. The directives espoused by *Humanae vitae* were not only to a large extent not accepted, they were actually rejected. As a foundation of what is natural and inherent in all human beings, biology as such just is not an adequate ethical or theological criterion. The human being as a person, endowed with conscience and responsibility, is more and other than a simply biologically-determined being. And that is true also in the area of sexuality.

Because the argumentation supporting *Humanae vitae* still put forth today—namely, that the language of nature is likewise the language of morality, and that to respect the biological is to respect God and therefore to defend God's creation[1]—is not convincing; it cannot gain support. Should one not instead perceive in the behavior of these most loyal Catholics a kind

1. Johannes Ratzinger, *Zur Lage des Glaubens. Ein Gespräch mit Vittorio Messori* (Munich–Zürich–Vienna, 1985) 98.

of *sensus fidelium,* which cannot simply be shunted aside? Peter Hünermann has said:

> When an extremely large number of committed Christian married people, after very careful investigation and examination of conscience and thoughtful consideration of the circumstances, use methods of contraception, this may be a sign of the *sensus fidelium,* of the loyal sense of the faith of the People of God, and not simply a symptom of an accommodation to the spirit of the times, to the *Zeitgeist,* or an overall defection from the faith.[2]

In the face of the unrest arising from *Humanae vitae* the bishops of West Germany, Austria, and Switzerland as well as the United States issued declarations which did not disavow but rather welcomed the encyclical, especially in its positive statements, but raised the issue of the responsible judgment of conscience in the concrete decisions of marriage partners. Now an attempt is being made to appear to forget these declarations and make them inoperative. Today they would no longer be possible or imaginable. Attempts are made to view declarations like those of the German bishops at Königstein in 1968 as mistaken and to annul them.

The General Synod of West Germany (1971–75) had as its goal the application and inculturation of the Second Vatican Council in the German Catholic Church in light of the new problems expressed so turbulently at the 1968 *Katholikentag* in Essen. It was only with great effort that Cardinal Döpfner could read out a greeting from the Pope. At that time a plan was formed to prepare and convene a General Synod of all the West German dioceses. The idea of such a synod was suggested by the Council itself, which had recalled the idea of a universal priesthood and the responsibility of all the faithful in the fulfillment of the mandate transmitted to the Church, and which had made people conscious of the unity of the ecclesiastical mission and the participation of all members of the people of God in the Church's mission and in the threefold office of Christ. The Synod of Würzburg, composed of bishops, priests,

2. Peter Hünermann, ''Droht eine dritte Modernismuskrise?'' *Herder-Korrespondenz* 43 (1989) 134.

theologians, members of religious orders, and laity, was an unparalleled center of communication, the experience and exchange of a lively *Communio* within the People of God, who together sought and discovered solutions through dialogue and reasoning based on faith.

Certainly the Synod also had its ups and downs; there were tensions that sometimes became an endurance test, expressions of a potential plurality in the Church. But the net did not break. The goodwill and commitment to the Church of all the participants were acknowledged. That created a solid base for community. Even the compromises which often had to be settled for were a sign of mutual respect. This is not the place to present the themes and conclusions of this Synod. The ''official complete edition''[3] provides this information. Especially impressive is the Synod's basic statement and its declaration, *Our Hope. A Declaration of Faith for This Time.* It is in a decisive way the work of Johannes B. Metz and bears his stamp in form and content. The initial draft was not infrequently disputed vehemently, ostensibly because of its one-sidedness, but it was in the end passed by a large majority. It is a text which today is still as moving, fresh, and encouraging as it was during the Synod itself.

The president of the General Synod, Julius Cardinal Döpfner, explained at the end of the final plenary assembly in November 1975:

> The Synod is over—the Synod begins. The real task, to fulfill with spirit and life what was deliberated and resolved in Würzburg, still lies before us. I hope the publication of this complete edition will be an aid in enabling the spirit and letter of the Synod's conclusions under the guidance of God's Spirit in the Church to assume a concrete and fruitful form on all levels in the Church of our country. It was this greatness of faith, hope and charity that the General Synod wished to serve. It is by this goal that the entire post-Synod work of practical translation must be inspired.[4]

3. *Gemeinsame Synode der Bistümer in der Bundesrepublik Deutschland* 1: *Beschlüsse der Vollversammlung. Offizielle Gesamtusgabe* (Freiburg–Basel–Vienna, 1976, 6th printing 1985).

4. Ibid., 8.

The General Synod in Würzburg had as its goal the
resumption of the Council and its inculturation in Germany.
It was sometimes referred to as the "German Council." The
closing song of the Synod was not "See a House Full of
Glory," but rather "Awake, the Voice Calls Us!"
The Synod has since faded from memory even more than
the Council itself. Scarcely any of the great expectations have
been fulfilled. In fact, it has come to the point where those who
cite the Synod today and draw upon it as an authority and
focus of the Catholic Church in Germany arouse suspicion in
some circles that they no longer stand upon the firm ground
of the Catholic Church of the present day, that they mourn
for something which even during its day was regarded with
mistrust, not least because in the voting and passing of reso-
lutions the Synod as a whole was acting as the representative
of the people of God in the *Bundesrepublik.*

Add to this that the decisions agreed upon by the Synod
were for the most part rejected by Rome, including even the
granting of permission to hold a synod every ten years. That
was not very encouraging, but until now it has been understood to mean that only diocesan synods may take place, as
in the diocese of Rottenburg-Stuttgart. The Würzburg Synod
was not only referred to in its *acta* but it remained extremely
influential in many of the Rottenburg-Stuttgart declarations.[5]

Suffering from the Church thus has its base in the *discrepancy between the Church of the Council* and the Würzburg
Synod and the *Church of the present,* between that which was
and that which is today. This suffering to be sure can be cor-
rectly understood and weighed only by one for whom the
Council and Synod are still living and present, who has found
in the Council and Synod a foundational orientation for Christian faith and life and for the form of the Church and who can
therefore draw a comparison.

Following are a few concrete examples of suffering from the
Church today.

5. Heinrich Fries, "Was bleibt von der Synode?" *Glaube und Kirche
im ausgehenden 20. Jahrhundert* (Munich, 1979) 154–165; "*Beschlüsse der Diö-
zesansynode Rottenburg-Stuttgart 1985/86,*" *Weitergabe des Glaubens an die kom-
mende Generation* (Ostfildern, 1986).

3 Renewal or Restoration?

Pope John XXIII had set a goal for the Council: It is not the task of this Council simply to repeat and emphasize the old truths of faith in the customary manner—there is no need of a Council for that—but rather to mediate the Gospel for the people of our day so that its message is simultaneously true to its origin and appropriate to the situation. That is not simple; it requires a leap from shore to shore, from then to now. Only in this way are Christian faith and its contents protected from becoming a superstructure, an ideology, a relic of the past or an alien thing. At the same time this defining of goals guarantees continuity and thus the identity of faith. Nothing, says the confessional statement of the Synod concerning faith in this time, requires as much loyalty as constant change.[6]

This task and insight lead to the defining of the Church as *ecclesia semper reformanda,* as a Church which is always both in need of and capable of renewal.

Today it is *restoration* rather than renewal which is being demanded, and this not as an essential effort to protect the irrevocable but as a return to a historical situation in which the Church was allegedly at peace within itself and stable, when it had for every problem a relevant and clear answer according to which the community of Catholic faithful regulated itself and which they themselves welcomed. The Church understood itself earlier as an imperturable rock against the floods of the ages, as a widely shining sign for all peoples. What the First Vatican Council had to say of the Church is clear from the following text:

6. *Gemeinsame Synode* (see note 3) 85.

Only the Catholic Church bears all the many wonderful signs which God has given so that the credibility of Christian teaching shines forth. Indeed, even of itself the Church is a great and constant argument for its authenticity and an irrefutable witness to its divine mission by virtue of its wonderful propagation, its outstanding sanctity and inexhaustible fruitfulness in all good things, in its catholic unity and unconquerable constancy. It follows that it is like a sign raised among the nations (Isa 11:12) inviting those who do not yet believe, which, however, gives to her children a firmly established certainty that their faith which they profess rests on a most secure foundation.[7]

Here we hear an ecclesiological triumphalism which strikes us today as distressing and out of place. A restoration to such a pattern is surely an absolute impossibility. At an earlier time, so it is said today, people had the courage to fix limits for themselves, to speak of heresy and schism, to identify and to condemn errors and even to punish mistaken developments. People knew what was Catholic. Only in this way, it is thought, can we protect the unity of the Catholic Church in the present and future. This is the more likely to be achieved, it is added today, the more that unity is perceived as a comprehensive uniformity, the more it is seen to be based on the principle of unity in the Petrine office and is controlled and determined from there, the more the windows and doors of the Church are closed to any draft from outside. That is happening today.

One principle of the Council was *Aggiornamento*. This does not means accommodating to the present time and *Zeitgeist*, for that would be conformity. *Aggiornamento* means the contemporaneity of faith. This includes paying attention to the signs of the times which, as the Council explained, are a theological locus that can and should be interpreted in light of the Gospel. The content of faith should be mediated through the reality of the world and the experiences of people, using their categories of thought and understanding, their questions and searches. Answers for which there are no questions or for

7. J. Neuner and H. Roos, *Der Glaube der Kirche in den Urkunden der Lehrverkündigung* (Freiburg: Herder, 1938) Nr. 385.

which the questions are not asked fly off into the blue, no matter how correct they are.

Today we see a tendency to present the truths of faith primarily in the articulation of formulated principles of faith and legal norms, and to make orthodoxy, true teaching, the one and only measure of faith. It is thought that the mediating and handing on of the faith can best be guaranteed by catechisms and the knowledge of the faith preserved therein. At the same time great value is placed on the contents, the material completeness of the doctrine. The important conciliar statement on the hierarchy and ranking of truths on the basis of their essential quality and their differing significance for salvation, a ranking which gives shape to the faith, fades into the background. The same is true of the basic structure of faith described in the Council as a free surrender of the entire person to God (*Dei verbum*), and also true of the transition of the faith from faith in knowledge to faith in experience, from faith in propositions to faith in trust, from faith in obedience to faith in understanding, a change which can be observed in current theology.[8]

The various new catechisms are supposed to serve orthodox dogma; they are expected to culminate in the world catechism, a symbol of unity as uniformity. The most recent Roman decree serves the same goal. Since March 1, 1989, Pope John Paul II has prescribed for Catholic clergy as well as those laypeople active in teaching and pastoral care a special loyalty oath to be taken on assumption of office, a new *professio fidei*. It takes the place of the anti-modernist oath of 1910[9] which was suspended in 1967, and includes the obligation to follow the teaching of the Church in word and deed, to heed its laws as well

8. E. Biser, ''Der Spiegel des Glaubens,'' *Münchener Theologische Zeitschrift* 39 (1988), 230; J. Werbick, *Glauben lernen aus Erfahrung* (Munich, 1989).

9. J. Neuner and J. Dupuis, *The Christian Faith in the Doctrinal Documents of the Catholic Church* (Dublin: Mercier Press, 1973) Nr. 143; Denzinger-Schönmetzer, *Enchiridion Symbolorum, Definitionum et Declarationum de Rebus Fidei et Morun* (Freiburg: Herder, 1962), Nr. 3537–3550. For the new oath, see *L'Osservatore Romano* February 25, 1989, 7, and *Herder-Korrespondenz* 43 (1989) 153f.

as to obey the bishops and the authentic teaching office. This new oath is intended to serve the unity of faith and unity in faith. Whether it does or can fulfill these expectations remains for the future to decide. It can be doubted, however.

Certainly it should not be denied that to know and to understand the contents of this faith is decisive for the faith and its transmission. Belief itself demands insight and comprehension appropriate to the connection between faith and discernment so often documented in the Gospel of John and in conformity with the classical principle of theology, *fides quaerens intellectum*, faith demanding insight and understanding for its own sake. In this way it is protected from misunderstanding and alienation.

But more important than the power coming from the truth of the faith and Christian teaching is the power coming from the *witness of a life of faith* as a testimony to the fruits of faith, especially in the form of the imitation of Jesus with its culmination in deeds of a radical and selfless love, especially in the service of the poorest of our sisters and brothers. Even though it has been said so often, it remains true: the works of Mother Teresa in Calcutta, her selfless care of the dying who have no one else, the orthopraxis they experience through her, this quiet service of innumerable Christians in the service of sick, suffering, lonely old people has been and continues to be more effective for the conveying of Christian faith in the Church than many sermons, lessons and theologies. Instinctively people ask, what brings people to act in this way?

Just as convincing is the radiant power which streams from many third world Churches, especially from the base communities there. If according to a familiar saying people are the only Bible which is still read today, one can infer how much depends on the witness of Christian life. That is also true of a Church as a community of faith and the faithful if it is, as today, an advocate for humans, their rights and values, making itself the voice of the voiceless, and commits itself to justice and peace, to overcoming terror and force, and when, by being a place of freedom within totalitarian states and systems, it stands up against structures which make it impossible to realize life in freedom. Here there is no cause for suffering from today's Church. Here the Church is credible to itself and to the entire world. Such an intervention becomes the more convincing as the Church itself becomes just and fair in similar claims and demands within.

4 *"Isms" or Real People?*

One characteristic of the Second Vatican Council was its turn toward real concrete people who are always much more than representatives of some kind of "ism." The modern Councils—Trent and Vatican I—were directed against the many forms of what were considered anti-faith and anti-Church isms: Protestantism, atheism, pantheism, agnosticism, materialism, communism. People were categorized within these systems, more or less identified with them and judged accordingly, and this for the most part led to condemnation. The Second Vatican Council, which deliberately did not formulate any dogma, tried to be a *pastoral Council,* a Council with ministerial intent. Earlier the Church perceived itself as surrounded by massive worldwide antagonism and withdrew into itself to defend and maintain itself. Vatican II neither belittled nor glorified the present situation, but unlike earlier Councils it kept the concrete person especially in mind: it was a "Council for." It dealt with the phenomenon of atheism, for example, in nuanced fashion. It inquired into the forms and shapes of atheism and what are possibly widely differing motives.[10] Atheism, as Karl Rahner once put it, can be a question clothed in an answer, the question being "Where are you, God?" Christians and the Churches, according to the Council, also share blame for the emergence of atheism.

According to the Council, however, the Church simply invites everyone to evaluate the Gospel of Jesus Christ dispassionately. The Council was convinced that the message of the faith corresponds to the deepest desires of the human heart and that even today people are in principle open to the mes-

10. *Gaudium et spes,* Nr. 21.

sage of faith and the words of Jesus Christ when these are effectively conveyed.

Today one gets the impression from the stipulations and measures of ecclesiastical authorities that axioms and principles, indispensable as they are, are more important than real people in a real situation. That can be seen, for example, in the question of the admission of innocent divorced and remarried people to the sacraments, in the treatment of priests who have withdrawn from office for a wide variety of motives; it can be seen in the general ban on Eucharistic hospitality and lay preaching during the Eucharistic celebration; it is seen recently in the inflexibility of the Pope on the question of contraception. His latest statement tends to reject the faithful's trust in their conscience, as if only the Teaching Office were competent on this question. The moral norm laid down by him "admits no exception. No personal or social circumstances would ever, can now, or will ever, render such an act lawful in itself."[11]

This statement does not fall within the category of papal decisions of an infallible teaching office.

Hans Küng's famous and highly debated book *Infallible? An Inquiry*[12] took the encyclical *Humanae vitae* as its starting point. This position was properly rejected both by the official ecclesiastical side and Catholic theology because the encyclical itself did not fall into the category of "infallible." If one considers the current statements of the papal teaching office on the value and significance of *Humanae vitae*—with no exceptions permitted and any calling upon conscience rejected—then one must agree with Peter Hünermann when he calls it "downright ghastly how far Rome was entered into the interpretation imputed by Hans Küng."[13]

11. *Con viva* (12 Nov 1988), "Truth in the Magisterium" (Address of Pope John Paul II to the Second International Congress on Moral Theology which was held to mark the twentieth anniversary of "Humanae Vitae") *The Pope Speaks*, 34, 2 (1989) 100.

12. Hans Küng, *Infallible? An Inquiry* (New York: Doubleday, 1972); see also Leonard Swidler, ed., *Küng in Conflict* (New York: Doubleday, 1981).

13. "Droht eine dritte Modernismuskrise?" (see note 2) 134.

The Pope's statement on *conscience* can have referred only to a very superficial, though of course widely propagated, understanding of conscience as the attitude of Catholics who did not care at all about statements of the Church's teaching office but used trust in conscience as an alibi for their own arbitrariness. However, from the misuse of conscience one may not draw any conclusions concerning its well-founded and responsible use. Conscience is not an empty slate which must first be inscribed; it enables people to know good and evil, right and wrong, and is at the same time a categorical imperative to do good. After a deed is accomplished conscience is an incorruptible judge. According to Paul, the law given by God to Israel through Moses is written in the hearts of humans, who do not recognize it as law but "are led by reason to do what the law commands" (Rom 2:14). It can then be said that conscience as a cry and a sound is simultaneously in me and above me. Here too it is true that the possible misuse of conscience does not reduce its significance and authority.

The statements of the ecclesiastical teaching office, though important, are not the only component in the formation and decision of conscience, and they are no substitute for conscience itself. On the same occasion Pope John Paul II said:

> Conscience, in fact, is the "place" where man is illuminated by a light which does not come to him from his created and always fallible reason, but from the very Wisdom of the Word in whom all things were created. "Conscience," as Vatican II again admirably states, "is a man's most secret core, and his sanctuary. There he is alone with God whose voice echoes in his depths."[14]

It is difficult to square this statement of the Pope with the one claiming that in the matter of contraception there can be no recourse to conscience and that there is no exception to this prohibition.

Newman's famous phrase, "Conscience first, Pope afterwards,"[15] is not intended to play off the two forces against each

14. "Truth in the Magisterium," 99.
15. John Henry Newman, *A Letter Addressed to His Grace the Duke of Norfolk, (on the occasion of) Mr. Gladstone's Recent Expostulation* (New York: The Catholic Publication Society, 1875) 86.

other or put them in opposition to one another, but rather to express an inner coordination and at the same time make clear that there is a final obligation and a primacy of conscience which must be obeyed even if, considered objectively, it were to be defined as erroneous. That is traditional Church teaching, initially formulated by Paul (Rom 14:25), explicitly repeated by Thomas Aquinas and John Henry Newman, and proclaimed by the Second Vatican Council. Newman said that "did the Pope speak against Conscience . . . he would commit a suicidal act. He would be cutting the ground from under his feet."[16]

16. Ibid., 77.

5   Dialogue or Monologue?

From these most recent statements of the Teaching Office it becomes clear that, instead of dialogue and communication between the Teaching Office and theology recommended at the Council, *monologue* and the *obligation of obedience* have come to the fore, that a strict compliance with the directions of the Teaching Office is considered the supreme virtue for Catholics as well as the criterion for Church membership. This is all the more problematic when from the very revelation which is entrusted to the Church and its authority there is nothing to be learned about the concrete questions of problems like birth control which have become acute only in our own day. Such questions can then not be elevated to the level of revealed truth. Just how problematic reference to human nature is becomes clear when nature is understood from a strictly biological view which overlooks the fact that human nature is determined by intellect, will, and freedom of decision and thus achieves a greater scope of freedom than determination by biology alone permits. Our contemporary existence, culture, and civilization, the advances of contemporary medicine rest upon a variety of intrusions into, and/or utilization of nature for persons.

The consequences which an alleged defense of human nature can lead to are shown in the express prohibition in the past century of smallpox vaccination as an invasion of God's Providence.

It is, however, not at all the case that *authority* as such is universally rejected today. It is accepted and even welcomed when it argues convincingly on the basis of the insights of faith and proves itself competent. But whenever and wherever authority haughtily appeals to itself alone and forbids further questions and discussions, its directives encounter resistance;

they will not be accepted, to the great damage of authority itself. Here there arises that polarization in the Church so deplored today. Bernard Häring has spoken of a psychological schism manifest today; on the one side the triumphalism of the intransigents, on the other side anger, mistrust, an anti-Roman feeling. As a result, came the distancing and sometimes departure of many from the Church. Add to this a climate in which hostility, denunciation, and accusations of heresy threaten to destroy completely whatever trust still remains. It all leads to the self-destruction of authority.

The authorities in the Church are themselves destroying its authority. Through their action or inaction they are causing trust to disappear and with it the presuppositions which alone can assure recognition and loyalty. Thus summons to obedience or other attempts at discipline are of no use whatsoever. They only aggravate the problem and contribute to the fact that more and more people are turning away from the Church in its contemporary condition.[17]

17. W. Seibel, ''Selbstzerstörung der Autorität,'' *Stimmen der Zeit* 14 (1989) 145.

6 The Primacy of the Pope and the College of Bishops

The Second Vatican Council, in supplementing the First Vatican Council which had defined only the doctrine of the primacy of the pope and the infallibility of his extraordinary teaching office, spelled out a doctrine concerning bishops, the college of bishops and the significance of dioceses and local churches. These moves did not in any way curtail the decisions of Vatican I. To be sure, Vatican I had already declared that the primacy of the pope did not detract from the office and authority of the bishops as successors to the apostles, that it was rather a task of the pope to strengthen the episcopal office and authority.[18]

The German bishops understood Bismarck and, with him, Gladstone, to interpret the decision of the First Vatican Council thus: ''The episcopal jurisdiction has disappeared into the papal.'' ''The pope . . . has in principle stepped into the place of every single bishop and it depends only on him whether he will at any single moment put himself in their position regarding governments in practice as well.'' ''The bishops are still only his tools, his officials without responsibility.'' ''They have become in relation to civil governments the officials of a foreign sovereign, and indeed of one who in virtue of his infallibility is a complete and absolute monarch, more than an absolute monarch of the world.''[19]

The German bishops, on the other hand, stated in a joint declaration of February 1875:

18. Denzinger-Schönmetzer, Nr. 3061.
19. Denzinger-Schönmetzer, Nr. 3113–3116.

All these statements ignore the foundation of, and stand in contradiction to, the text, as well as the correct meaning of the conclusions of the Vatican Council as repeatedly explained by the pope, the episcopacy and the representatives of Catholic scholarship.

Furthermore, the conclusions of the Vatican Council offer no least justification for the assertion that through them the pope has become an absolute monarch, and indeed by virtue of his infallibility a "perfectly absolute monarch more than any kind of absolute monarch in the world." First of all the area to which the ecclesiastical dominion of the pope refers is essentially different from that to which the worldly sovereignty of the monarch refers; the full sovereignty of local princes over Catholics in the *civil* area is nowhere disputed. But even apart from this the description of an absolute monarch in reference to *ecclesiastical affairs* cannot be applied to the pope because he stands under divine law and is bound by the rules set by Christ for his Church. The pope cannot alter the structure given the Church by its divine founder as a secular lawgiver can alter a civil structure. The organization of the Church rests in all essential points upon divine direction and is removed from any human choices.

On the strength of the same divine institution on which the papacy rests the episcopacy also stands firm; it too has its rights and duties by virtue of the order set by God which the pope has neither the right nor the power to change. It is therefore a complete misunderstanding of the Vatican decrees to believe that through them "episcopal jurisdiction has disappeared into the papal," that the pope has "in principle stepped into the place of every single bishop," that the bishops are "only the tools of the pope, his officials without responsibility". . . . Especially this [last] assertion . . . we can only reject with all firmness; it is truly not the Catholic Church in which the immoral and despotic principle that the command of the superior is unconditionally binding on its own authority has found acceptance.

Finally the opinion that the pope is "by virtue of his infallibility a complete and absolute sovereign" rests on a complete misconception of the dogma of papal infallibility. As the Vatican Council said clearly and distinctly, and as the nature of the matter itself reveals, the dogma refers solely to an attribute of the supreme papal *Teaching Office*: this covers precisely the same area as the infallible teaching office of the Church in general and is linked to the contents of Holy Scripture and Tradition as well as the dogmatic decisions already made by the ecclesiastical teaching office. With regard to the governing actions of the pope there results thereby not the least change.[20]

Pope Pius IX approved this declaration of the German bishops completely and entirely as the correct interpretation. The Catholic Church has once again become a *Papal Church,* more intensively today than ever before. The primacy of the pope and his infallibility *ex cathedra* defined by Vatican I is used in an extensive, completely unlimited fashion and has been expanded into all areas. The International Episcopal Synods as representative of the collegiality of the bishops have only an advisory character—what comes out is handed over entirely to the judgment of the pope. He made use of this in the post-synodical statement *Christifideles laici* (December 30, 1988). The national Episcopal Conferences of various countries have likewise no competence as such; they are advisory groups for the individual bishop who can make use of the conference as he likes. Today we are experiencing throughout the Church a *centralization* and a *regimentation* which proceed from Rome and take practically everything in the Church under their jurisdiction, making decisions from Rome outward. Unity in variety, legitimate though it be, is seen as a danger.

The *communio* structure of the Church stressed in Vatican II is as good as smothered by this practice. *Communio,* however, needs *communication,* dialogue, and cooperation, or it is no longer credible. The present understanding and practice of the papacy, seen from an ecumenical perspective, is no longer communicable. All the efforts of non-Catholic theologians to approach the papacy as the Petrine office and to see in it a sign and instrument of unity in truth and love, as was the case with Pope John XXIII, are blocked by this new praxis.

The attitude described above is nowhere as striking as in the current worldwide practice of naming bishops, who occupy a decisive key position in the Church. These appointments are perceived as being made apart from the principle of *commu-*

---

20. Denzinger-Schönmetzer, Nr. 3113–3116.

nio, from the collegiality of bishops and the local Church and as having been taken over by the pope and *curia* alone.

Examples from the Netherlands, Austria, Switzerland, and Germany, but also from the Churches in the Third World, document this before the entire public.

Canon 377 of the *Codex Iuris Canonici* states: "The Supreme Pontiff freely appoints or confirms those who have been legitimately elected." This raises the question, "Who are legitimately elected, and how?"

History provides many models. Earlier the bishop was chosen by the clergy and the people. Pope Leo I (440–461) established the principle: Whoever wishes to preside over all must be elected by all.

In the course of history the issue of electing bishops and naming bishops often resulted in a struggle between secular and spiritual power in the Church, especially as many bishops were also secular rulers. At a time when princes and kings often made choices to suit their own interests it was perceived as liberating when the pope in the name of freedom of the Church assumed the task of naming bishops on his own authority.

But these conditions no longer exist in the free world. In modern times there are rules which have been mutually agreed upon in concordats. But today one gets the impression that such stipulations are more and more seen as a hindrance and therefore repressed in favor of an unlimited free decision-making power of the pope. Certainly the freedom mentioned here cannot be abandoned when it pertains to the freedom of the Church concerning interference by state agencies, perhaps by a totalitarian anti-Church government. But this charge cannot validly be made against those democratic governments which acknowledge the freedom and independence of the Church and even concede both privilege and assistance to the Church.

From a formal juridical point of view Rome can point to the fact that, for example, it presented a list to Cologne and to Salzburg from which the cathedral chapters could choose a candidate—a list which, however, having entirely passed over the list first submitted by the Cologne cathedral chapter, was made up of completely new names. Thus free choice was highly problematic. If the choice was limited to this list, it was felt, the nomination fell to the pope as the highest authority. There can therefore be no accusation of breaking the concordat. But such formal legal correctness overlooks the fact that in the naming of a bishop what is of primary concern is that the man chosen be the one who best fulfills the prerequisites for the office of bishop, who knows the local Church, knows its mission, possibilities, and problems and will be accepted and welcomed by the people. Delegations from Salzburg who went to Rome with this intent in order to discuss the matter were never received.

If, however, by a change in the voting laws during the actual election process Rome names as bishop a man who until then had absolutely no relationship to the local Church, it damages the entire Church, which consists completely of local churches. The criterion currently set in Rome for the naming of a bishop is the complete conformity of the candidate to the praxis in force in Rome. The supreme virtue for him is unlimited obedience to Rome, particularly on the question of *Humanae vitae*. Hans Maier, for many years the president of the Central Committee of German Catholics, spoke not long ago of the "crop damage" produced by the current method of naming bishops.

A similar centralism and regimentation can be seen in the *appointment of theology professors.* Although not the case earlier, they now need the *Nihil obstat* conferred by Rome; where this is lacking an appointment by the state is likewise impossible. That of course signifies a vote of no-confidence in the local Churches.

It is difficult to understand why the bishops handed over their authority and duties on the appointment of professors.

In this context it should also be noted that in the Lefebvre case Rome exercised patience and showed a willingness to make concessions which went to extreme, scarcely justifiable limits. That Lefebvre nevertheless did break away from Rome must be considered no less than tragic.

On the other hand, in the case of those theology professors who expressly affirm the Council and Church but occasionally bring up a few theses or hypotheses which are somewhat daring but nevertheless suitable for discussion, quite different measures are taken. They lose their teaching positions, and a ban on writing or speaking is imposed on them; they are forced, as in the era of Modernism, to show obedience and compliance.

The reproach of "Modernism" is making an appearance lately like a ghost of the old Modernist-hunt. There is no lack of collaborators and informers. Spies sit in on some professorial lectures and hand in reports.

7 *Ecumenism*

Vatican II was an ecumenical council not only as defined by Catholic Church law but also insofar as the Council made ecumenical concerns its own. It expressed repentance over divisions in the Church and made an effort to bring them to an end. In great contrast to its earlier manner of thought and conduct the Catholic Church, which had suspected, repudiated, and forbade any ecumenical contact, now moved into the ecumenical movement with a clear consciousness that the continuing division was a growing scandal to the world, a scandal which made the Gospel message incredible. The Council saw the path to Christian unity in the renewal of the Church, which should have as its orientation the Gospel and profound reflection on the Church's mission.

In the sixteenth century reform and reformation were the program which led to the separation of the Churches and Christians in the West; today they are the path to oneness through unification. One discovers more and more that what is common to the Churches is greater and deeper than their differences; this leads one to reflect today on whether these differences must forever remain a basis of separation. Can they instead be building blocks in the structure of a conciliatory diversity? On this matter current ecumenical dialogues are moving on various levels and in various spheres.[21] Moreover the Council, and even more the Würzburg Synod, considered what might be done together in the area of prayer and worship, in the sphere of instruction and formation, and especially

---

21. See Karl Lehmann and Wolfhart Pannenberg, eds., *Lehrverur-teilungen-kirchentrennend? Rechtfertigung, Sakramente und Amt in Zeitalter der Reformation und Heute* (Freiburg-Göttingen, 1968, 3rd ed., 1988).

in the province of service and charity. Often it is more than we suspect and more than we can accomplish.

Ecumenism has become an opportunity and challenge for all of Christianity. It can no longer be undone. Ecumenism goes on, even if no longer with the same forcefulness it had during the Council. But it is an everyday reality, which confirms the accomplishments of the Council.

It has to be said that more has been achieved ecumenically in the post-conciliar period than had been for centuries. What is taken for granted today was unimaginable thirty years ago. On this matter one must consider how to evaluate the present ecumenical situation and to recognize in it a basis for further hope. Because the number of still unresolved questions continues to decrease, there is no reason for discouragement.

Currently we have an ecumenism of statements of commitment, a more intensive form of which can hardly be imagined. As an example we can take the statement Pope John Paul II made at his departure from Munich in 1980:

> I wish to serve unity; I wish to walk all the ways in which, after the experiences of the centuries and millennia, Christ is leading us toward the unity of that flock where he alone is the *only and reliable Good Shepherd.* . . . I hold the firm hope that the *unity of Christians is already on its way* in the power of the Spirit of truth and love. We know how long the times of separation and division have been. But we do not know how long the way to unity will be. One thing we know with all the greater certainty: *We have to keep on walking this way with perseverance*—keep on going and not stand still! There are many things we have to do for it; above all, we have to *persevere in prayer in an ever more powerful and intimate prayer.* Unity can be given only as a gift of the Lord, as the fruit of his passion and resurrection, in the ''fullness of time'' appointed to it.[22]

The Pope has corroborated this statement in his many meetings with representatives of various Christian Churches.

Nevertheless it must be said that the words of solemn commitment do not correspond to *concrete praxis.*

22. *L'Osservatore Romano* (English edition), December 22, 1980, 11; Vol. 51, 663 of the Italian edition.

One has the impression that the postconciliar attitude of the Catholic Church is defined by the principle "thus far and no further." The movement visible in the Council turns into boundary markers which form an impediment to any further ecumenical steps.

This becomes clear in the question of community in worship and Communion in common, the object of a worldwide ecumenical longing.

The Council laid down two principles for a solution to this question: Christ instituted "the wonderful sacrament of the Eucharist by which the unity of the Church is both signified and brought about."[23] Community in worship (including shared Eucharist) "should signify the unity of the Church; it should provide a sharing in the means of grace. The fact that it should signify unity generally rules out common worship. Yet the gaining of a needed grace sometimes commends it. The practical course to be adopted, after due regard has been given to all the circumstances of time, place, and personage, is left to the prudent decision of the local episcopal authority. . . .'"[24]

Since the Council, the emphasis in the Catholic Church has shifted to the extent that almost only one aspect receives much attention. Shared Eucharist is an expression of communion in faith and therefore can occur only if this unity in faith is achieved. The other aspect, that Eucharist as participation in the source of grace makes Eucharistic community acceptable in individual cases, is scarcely mentioned now. And yet this very principle would be a help in many concrete cases. The actual decision is a question of conscience involving careful analyses of one's responsibility, the given situation and the possible consequences. The Würzburg Synod explicitly alluded to this and to the ecumenical potential and widened the possibility "from a keyhole opening to a door ajar."[25]

The principle that the Eucharist is an expression of community in faith, and thus possible only at the end of the road, had already been demolished when after the Council the Catholic Church offered Eucharistic fellowship to the Ortho-

23. *Unitatis redintegratio,* Nr. 2.
24. Ibid., Nr. 8.
25. "Beschluss Gottesdienst," *Gemeinsame Synode,* 780f.

dox Churches. In fact, those Churches reject such important Catholic items of faith as the primacy of the pope, the infallibility of his teaching office, and the newer Marian dogmas, and for their part they are not open to Eucharistic fellowship. It must therefore be asked: To what extent must there be unity in faith before shared Eucharist is possible? Here the German Protestant Church has a more open regulation. It grants Eucharistic community to all who are open to it and find themselves inwardly moved to it. And this, it is said, is completely consistent with loyalty to one's own Church.

But if Eucharistic community is defined as a complete accord of all the Churches with both the Roman Catholic Church and its dogma and canonical decisions, as Daniel Ols, a critic of the Rahner-Fries book who denies our Catholic orthodoxy, insists,[26] then the *Oikoumene* can be written off, for the other Churches are not ready for this. It would mean their unconditional capitulation. Only one solution is possible, that contained in the book *Unity of the Churches. An Actual Possibility*, published by Karl Rahner and myself: An agreement of the Churches in a faith based on Holy Scripture, the ancient confessions of faith, and the early Councils of a still undivided Church.

As for the teaching decisions and dogmas presented in the course of later faith history, especially as they have been enacted within the Catholic Church, the valid principle ought to be: None of these final dogmatic decisions may be rejected by another Church as contrary to the Gospel. That demands a high measure of willingness to take the extra step on the part of the other Churches. On the other hand, the non-Catholic Churches must not be constrained to accept these dogmas themselves; it is sufficient if they grant that such new dogmas are a legitimate development of the faith in one part of the Church. The Würzburg Synod expressly affirmed this principle,[27] as did Cardinal Ratzinger in his description of the relations between Rome and the Orthodox Churches:

26. *L'Osservatore Romano*, February 25/26, 1985; see also Heinrich Fries in Heinrich Fries and Otto Hermann Pesch, eds., *Streiten für eine Kirche* (Munich: Kösel Verlag, 1987) 61–67.
27. ''Beschluss Ökumene,'' in *Gemeinsame Synode*, 780f.

Certainly, no one who claims allegiance to Catholic theology can simply declare the doctrine of primacy null and void, especially not if he seeks to understand the objections and evaluates with an open mind the relative weight of what can be determined historically. Nor is it possible, on the other hand, for him to regard as the only possible form and, consequently, as binding on all Christians, the form this primacy has taken in the nineteenth and twentieth centuries. . . . In other words, Rome must not require more from the East with respect to the doctrine of primacy than had been formulated and was lived in the first millennium. . . . Reunion could take place in this context if, on the one hand, the East would cease to oppose as heretical the developments that took place in the West in the second millennium and would accept the Catholic Church as legitimate and orthodox in the form she had acquired in the course of that development, while, on the other hand, the West would recognize the Church of the East as orthodox and legitimate in the form she has always had.[28]

At the 1987 *Katholikentag* in Aachen, Richard von Weizsäcker, the West German President, said something that was badly received by some Catholics and even by bishops, but which in my opinion opened a continuing path and ought to be pondered by all the Churches. What he said can be an orientation and help:

The ecumenical movement has a chance not where people try to draw others to their own side but where they seek partners who are firmly anchored in their own faith. When the *Oikoumene* aids in a mutual strengthening of faith its credibility increases. It would be a gift if we were also reciprocally granted complete admission as guests to the Protestant liturgy and Catholic Mass. The right to hospitality is still not unity, which only God can grant us. But does someone who accepts a guest who is not a member of the family and really welcomes him or her encroach on God's jurisdiction? In considering hospitality neither the hosts nor the guests give up what is their own. But the remote moves near, the foreign is trusted, the stranger becomes the neighbor.

28. Cardinal Joseph Ratzinger, *Principles of Catholic Theology: Building Stones for a Fundamental Theology*, translated by Mary Frances McCarthy, S.N.D. (San Francisco: Ignatius Press, 1987) 198f.

This question of shared Communion or Eucharistic hospitality becomes especially acute as well as painful in the situation of an inter-confessional marriage, earlier referred to by the derogatory term ''mixed marriage.'' In the past this was considered a very great misfortune that could wound a family and for this reason people of all the Churches were expressly warned about such marriages. The Catholic Church forbade them in principle and allowed exceptions only with strict stipulations.

Despite all these warnings and prohibitions the number of inter-confessional marriages has constantly increased; today they include more than a third of those couples who still wish to have a church wedding; they have almost become the rule. This situation must not simply be deplored, nor should it be regulated as a matter of pure discipline. Instead everything must be done so that such marriages are not discriminated against or made the focus of constant insults and rejections or a cause of religious indifference or alienation from the Church. In the meanwhile much has happened between the Churches in the legal and pastoral areas to moderate the previous harshness. But the task is certainly not completed. An aid and a solution are possible only when such marriages become more and more a form and expression of *Oikoumene* in which communality in faith is realized and differences treated with respect. The partners can and should be mutually enriched. From confessionally-different marriages there should be more and more confessionally-unifying marriages.

The fact that partners in such marriages long for community in worship and Eucharist is an expression of their faith and love and in no way a sign of disobedient protest.

Such marriages show the conditions and presuppositions which are decisive for community in worship and Eucharist. No universal and undifferentiated rule can be drawn from this, but they do portray a concrete situation which enables a responsible decision of conscience.

In this way a variety of sufferings from the Church could be confronted in a helpful way.

In his new book, *United in Life—Divided in Confession. The Inter-confessional Marriage. Doctrine—Problems—Chances*, Peter Neuner says:

Inter-confessional marriage is also a sacrament and therefore must be understood as a "house-Church." From this perspective the question of eucharistic community in *interconfessional marriages* is seen in a new light. If eucharistic community and church community belong indissolubly together, as is constantly stressed on the Catholic side, then the interconfessional marriage must also be taken seriously as Church. It also is a figure of the fundamental sacrament, Church; in it likewise Church finds its existence. The inter-confessional marriage expresses Church, not Church-division. And for Church, according to fundamental Catholic conviction, Eucharist is indispensable and constitutive. This reflection could open a way for the Catholic Church, in complete loyalty to its dogmatic basic principles, to view a eucharistic community in inter-confessional marriages and families as legitimate. For the continuing confessional difference is encircled by the sacramentality of the marriage between baptized persons, who live in a "house-Church."[29]

29. *Geeint im Leben—getrennt im Bekenntnis. Die konfessionsverschiedene Ehe. Lehre—Probleme—Chancen* (Düsseldorf, 1989) 110f.

8 The Church as People of God

The Council's basic statement in its definition of the Church is its description of Church as People of God. With this the earlier narrowness which defined the Church by the hierarchy and understood ecclesiology as hierarchology has been overcome.

The Church defined as People of God sees itself as the community of those whose faith is oriented to Jesus Christ and whose lives are understood as an imitation of Christ; the principal feature of such a Church is *communio*.

The Council's statements on the hierarchy, especially the pope and bishops, conform to its statement on the People of God in order to make it very clear that office in the Church has no purpose of itself but exists as gift and service in coordinating the People of God. Office is for the People of God, not vice versa.

This itself moves the theme of *The Laity in the Church* into focus. Here the layperson is not perceived in a derogatory manner as the non-expert who understands nothing of matters of faith and Church and therefore needs to be led and instructed, as was customary for a long time, and not described simply as a non-cleric, as a subordinate to serve and to be served. "Layperson" is rather an honorable title referring to a member of the People of God, to which office and hierarchy also belong; the latter thus cannot be played off against the People of God.

The Council speaks of the laity in various connections. The notion of the priesthood of all the faithful (1 Pet 2:2-10), so vital in the Reformation and Reformation Churches to this very day, was taken up with vigor. The Council described the laity as all the faithful except those in holy orders and those in a religious state sanctioned by the Church. These faithful are by baptism made one body with Christ and are established among the People of God. They are in their own way made sharers in the priestly, prophetic, and kingly functions of Christ. They carry out their own part in the mission of the whole Christian people with respect to the Church and the world.[30]

The activity of the laity in the Church is no longer described as participation in the hierarchical apostolate as if the laity are at bottom only the extended arm of the clergy or the recipients of hierarchical commands. The mission of the laity is participation in the salvific mission of the Church in and for the world, for its proper function, form and order.

> But the laity, by their very vocation, seek the Reign of God by engaging in temporal affairs and by ordering them according to the plan of God. They live in the world, that is in each and in all of the secular professions and occupations. They live in the ordinary circumstances of family and social life, from which the very web of their existence is woven. They are called there by God so that by exercising their proper function and being led by the spirit of the Gospel they can work for the sanctification of the world from within, in the manner of leaven. In this way they can make Christ known to others, especially by the testimony of a life resplendent in faith, hope, and charity.

The laity have a special vocation in the state of marriage and family life. "The Christian family loudly proclaims both the present virtues of the Reign of God and the hope of a blessed life to come. Thus by its example and its witness it accuses the world of sin and enlightens those who seek the truth." It is expressly stated that "the laity are called in a special way to make the Church present and operative in those places and circumstances where only through them can she become the salt of the earth."[31]

The relationship between clergy and laity is described as follows: "Pastors of the Church, following the example of the Lord, should minister to one another and to the other faith-

30. *Lumen gentium*, Nr. 31.
31. Ibid., Nrs. 31, 35, 33.

ful. The faithful in their turn should enthusiastically lend their cooperative assistance to their pastors and teachers." For this reason the document also says, "Let sacred pastors recognize and promote the dignity as well as the responsibility of the laity in the Church."

"The laity have the right . . . to receive in abundance from their sacred pastors the spiritual goods of the Church, especially the assistance of the Word of God and the sacraments."

The chapter on the laity concludes with the moving words: "Each individual layperson must stand before the world as a witness to the resurrection and life of the Lord Jesus and as a sign that God lives."[32]

The question of the laity in the Church was the theme of an international episcopal synod in 1987, "The Vocation and Mission of the Laity in Church and World Twenty Years after Vatican II." Because international episcopal synods have only a consultative character for possible positions and decisions to be taken by the pope, the significance of this synod was limited from the beginning. That did not prevent this particular synod from producing extremely fruitful discussions as well as sharing a variety of experiences in the Church throughout the world. The point of origin and the orienting of the synod were the statements of the Council itself on the laity and the rejection of a definition of laity as non-clergy. The concept of the people and the principle of *communio* associated with it was emphatically stressed: a communality to which all distinctions are to be subordinated and from which perspective they also can and should be understood.

What the Council alluded to, the synod vigorously stressed: The task of the laity is ministry for the world, ministry to the possibilities, tasks, and challenges which today's Church sees confronting it! The task of office, on the other hand, can be described as salvific ministry. Such a distinction, however, is not helpful, because it is not relevant but instead creates a new polarization. There is no ecclesiastical ministry to the world to be attended to by the laity which can be separated from salvific ministry; ministry to the world is part of the basic commission of the entire people of God, and an unworldly salvific

32. Ibid., Nrs. 32, 37, 38.

ministry does not exist, for such ministry must be actualized in service to the world through service to Christians living in the world.

The pronouncement of Pope John Paul II, *Christifideles laici* (December 30, 1988), emphasized these basic ideas with great vigor. Today, the Pope said, the laity have taken upon themselves too many Church tasks and shown too little commitment to society and the world.

In current praxis we see a strong tendency to oppose any erosion of Church office and to call attention to its specific form: The priest ''can do'' what no layperson can. Fear of contact between office-bearers and laity in the service of the Church becomes more intense. Efforts are made to exclude the laity, especially the pastoral assistants and ''pastoral referents'' [lay professionals working full time in German Catholic parishes], who have had a complete theological education, from specifically pastoral functions in the parish and to assign them nonparochial tasks. The most significant example of this is the ban on lay preaching during the Eucharistic celebration in accordance with Canon 767.1. The authority of the bishops to dispense from this universal regulation, exercised in most German dioceses for more than fifteen years, was canceled by Rome. The Würzburg Synod had been concerned with this very issue and referred the matter to Rome in the form of a petition. It was rejected.

So-called lay preaching during the Eucharistic celebration is not simply an emergency measure compensating for the lack of priests. In the great majority of cases it was a genuine enrichment of the Church's mission of proclamation, especially when these laypeople, the pastoral referents, had a complete theological education. If, as the Council says, the laity have a share in the prophetic office of Jesus Christ, then it is not clear why this should not be valid for homilies during the Eucharistic celebration. The thesis that the mission of proclaiming the faith with teaching authority in the Church belongs to consecrated office-bearers while the laity have the mission of witnessing to the faith is not tenable. The solution suggested by the German Bishops Conference—a homily before the beginning of the liturgy with a suitable introduction by the celebrant—is the sign of a serious embarrassment which scarcely anyone comprehends or finds convincing. The prohibition decreed by Rome is a step backwards and shows a complete disregard for the situation in today's local Church for which the bishops bear the responsibility. It explicitly directs that the preaching commission of the laity remain outside the Eucharistic celebration.

In this context it is not surprising that attempts are made today to criticize the definition of Church as People of God. It is said that the concept is inadequate and vague and does not represent the reality of the relationship to Christ. The proper response is this: the definition of the Church as people of God is fully adequate if it is said that the Church is the people of *that* God who in Jesus Christ was conclusively communicated to the world and became human in it.

Talk of the people of God and the laity always includes both men and women. Nevertheless, the matter of *women in the Church* must still be dealt with specifically. Women were from the very beginning not only the most loyal of Jesus' disciples, standing beneath the cross and being the first witnesses to the resurrection, but women have been also the most loyal members of the people of God, the Church, throughout history.

Nevertheless it is a fact that today many women, especially younger women, reject and leave the Church. The significance of this for the next generation will be clear only later. Many women find that they are not accepted in the Church, that their rights, service and functions are not properly valued. The words of the Pauline epistles, ''Women are to remain quiet in the Church since they have no permission to speak'' (1 Cor 14:34), remain in effect to this very day. Too much remains reserved for men; women are excluded from whole areas of the Church. In this age of equality women are assuming almost all the positions in politics, art, scholarship, and business that earlier were the exclusive domain of men. If this is not possible in the ecclesiastical sphere, if woman's function is related primarily to her role in marriage and family or her service as a nun, then this creates unease and is for many a source of suffering from a Church which, it is said, has not understood the signs of the times.

The position of the Church can be seen as follows: Women's value and rights and their equality in the order of creation and salvation are expressed with the greatest possible emphasis. The apostolic doctrinal statement *Christifideles laici* says:

> In speaking about participation in the apostolic mission of the Church, there is no doubt that in virtue of Baptism and Confirmation, a woman—as well as a man—is made a sharer in the threefold mission of Jesus Christ, priest, prophet and king, and is thereby charged and given the ability to fulfill the fundamental apostolate of the Church: evangelization. However, a woman is called to put to work in this apostolate the "gifts" which are properly hers: first of all, the gift that is her very dignity as a person exercised in word and testimony of life, gifts therefore connected with her vocation as a woman.

Without explaining the relationship, the document immediately continues:

> In her participation in the life and mission of the Church a woman cannot receive the sacrament of Orders and therefore cannot fulfill the proper function of the ministerial priesthood. This is a practice that the Church has always found in the expressed will of Christ, totally free and sovereign, who called only men to be His apostles; a practice that can be understood from the rapport between Christ, the Spouse, and His bride, the Church. Here we are in the area of function, not of dignity and holiness. . . .
>
> However, as Pope Paul VI has already written, "We cannot change what our Lord did nor His call to women; but we can recognize and promote the role of women in the mission of evangelization and in the life of the Christian community."
>
> Above all, the acknowledgment in theory of the active and responsible presence of women in the Church must be realized in practice. . . .
>
> An example comes to mind in the participation of women in diocesan and parochial pastoral councils as well as diocesan synods and particular councils. In this regard the synod fathers have written: "Without discrimination, women should be participants in the life of the Church and also in consultation and the process of coming to decisions." And again: "Women, who already hold places of great importance in transmitting the faith and offering every kind of service in the life of the Church, ought

to be associated in the preparation of pastoral and missionary documents and ought to be recognized as cooperators in the mission of the Church in the family, in professional life and in the civil community."[33]

One must be allowed to ask whether the above call to the praxis of Jesus as seen in his call to the apostles is an irreversible norm valid for all time, excluding women from the so-called official priesthood, or whether the place of woman in society, which has since changed essentially, does not play a decisive role.

In today's Church we see immense efforts to admit women to the office of the diaconate and thus revive a praxis of the early Church which was largely forgotten.[34] The Würzburg Synod offered the following reasons:

> Many women in many regions of the Church, and not merely in mission areas, perform many of the activities which are part of the diaconal office. Exclusion of these women from ordination means a separation of function from sacramentally-mediated salvific power which cannot be justified either theologically or pastorally.
>
> A further reason lies in the fact that the position of woman in Church and society today makes it seem irresponsible to exclude her from pastorally desirable and theologically possible functions of office in the Church.
>
> Finally, with the inclusion of women in the sacramental diaconate we can expect in many respects an enrichment, both for the office as a whole and for the current development of the diaconate in particular.
>
> The diaconate is an independent expression of the sacrament of ordination which is theologically and functionally separate from the priestly ministry. The historical findings on the diaconate of women and on the priesthood of women differ. The question of the admission of women to the sacramental diaconate

33. *Christifideles laici* (Dec. 30, 1988), "The Vocation and Mission of the Lay Faithful in the Church and the World," *The Pope Speaks*, 34, 2 (1989) 153f.

34. See Virginia Ratigan and Arlene Swidler, eds., *A New Phoebe* (Kansas City: Sheed & Ward, 1990), for a contemporary discussion about initiating the diaconate for women in the Catholic Church today.

is therefore different from the question of the priesthood for women.

The basic equality of man and woman acknowledged in our society should lead us in the ecclesiastical area to matching pastoral and liturgical tasks for male and female deacons. Should, however, different focal points result in actual practice, that can serve a fruitful development of office. It does not, however, affect the basic equality of rights and duties.[35]

The Würzburg Synod sent a corresponding request to the pope. Until now it has not been accepted, but the problem persists. A mere veto is no solution.

35. "Beschluss Dienste und Ämter," *Gemeinsame Sunode*, 617. Concerning this entire topic see Peter Neuner, *Der Laie und das Gottesvolk* (Frankfurt, 1988).

9 The Church as "Mysterium"

Instead of the Church as People of God, today, especially since the extraordinary International Episcopal Synod of 1985,[36] the designation of the Church as *mysterium* is favored. This certainly reflects the proclamation of the Council in the first chapter of the Constitution on the Church, *Lumen gentium*. But the concept of *mysterium* as such is quite general to begin with and must be defined more precisely when considering the Church. *Mysterium* in the Council's sense means that "in Christ the Church is a kind of sacrament, that is, a sign of and instrument for the most intimate union with God, and for the unity of all humanity."

The description of the Church as *mysterium* would be misunderstood if it were linked to the idea that the Church is something enigmatic, incomprehensible, obscure, which exceeds human understanding and remains inaccessible, something which must not be touched but only venerated with amazement and faith and which soars like a secret power beyond everyday life. Church as *mysterium* would be equally misunderstood if one were of the opinion that it is carried aloft by the power of a higher intelligence. Progress in faith and thought consists rather of comprehending the mystery with ever greater depth.

Another way in which Church as *mysterium* might be misunderstood is if the term were used almost as a code word to prevent any concrete questions being put to the concrete Church, and instead hallowed and legitimated the status quo, all decisions and rules, made them in effect indisputable, and

36. See Walther Kasper, *Zukunft aus der Kraft des Konzils. Die ausserordentliche Bischofssynode '85. Die Dokumente mit einem Kommentar* (Freiburg: Herder, 1986).

surrounded them with the cloak of untouchable mystery. A Church understood in this way can admit no call to conversion and renewal, much less take seriously any criticism, for these would all be an attack on the Church as *mysterium*.

Even the Church's sin and failure, both in the present and the past, are affected, because they cannot be attributed to a *mysterium*. The Church's sin can be admitted only as a happy fault, a *felix culpa*. Suffering from the Church is once again dismissed through the *mysterium* Church.

If the designation of Church as *mysterium* thus becomes a refuge in which to hide when faced with pressing sorrows, problems, and tasks, a retreat still surrounded by the defenses of the incomprehensible and mysterious which fend off all questions, then calling the Church *mysterium* is not only incorrect but also dangerous and disastrous.[37]

---

37. See the chapter "Kirche als Mysterium" in: Heinrich Fries, *"Damit die Welt glaube"*. *Gefährdung-Ermutigung-Erneuerung* (Frankfurt, 1987) 249-263.

10 The Cologne Declaration

On January 6, 1989, a resolution prepared by a small circle of theology professors, ''Against the Muzzling—For an Open Catholicity,'' was issued. This document has since been signed by more than two hundred theologians and made public. The repercussions were extraordinarily great—the media had become involved—and, as was to be expected, opinions were divided. Alongside the affirmative responses, which made up the majority, there were negative voices as well. One cardinal in Rome declared that all the signers were heretics. There was also criticism from the German Bishops' Conference along with an acknowledgement of the legitimacy, even necessity, of an intra-church critique and with the important advice of Bishop Karl Lehmann that dialogue should take place concerning the relationship between the pastoral teaching office of the bishops and the mission and function of scholarly theology.

It must be remembered that the collaboration of bishops and theologians at the Second Vatican Council was a blessing which produced gratifying results in the conciliar texts; this was also true of the Würzburg Synod.

The Cologne Declaration is not the document of wild rebels or, as some supposed, a battle cry against pope and papacy. Church, Council and papacy were explicitly affirmed and their significance appreciated. That does not exclude, but rather assumes, that people may, and sometimes even must, take critical positions on certain principles and decisions of office in the Church, even up to the Petrine office of the pope. That is a service to this office.

The *Codex Iuris Canonici* says:

> In accord with the knowledge, competence and preeminence which they possess, they [the laity] have the right and even at times a duty to manifest to the sacred pastors their opinion on matters which pertain to the good of the Church, and they have a right to make their opinion known to the other Christian faithful, with due regard for the integrity of faith and morals and reverence toward their pastors, and with consideration for the common good and the dignity of persons (Can 212, 3).
>
> Those who are engaged in the sacred disciplines enjoy a lawful freedom of inquiry and of prudently expressing their opinions on matters in which they have expertise, while observing a due respect for the *magisterium* of the Church (Can 218).

This task is primarily a matter of the theology which the Church itself takes for granted, but theology does not simply repeat, corroborate or legitimize the decisions of the pastoral Teaching Office. Theology too has a role in the situation which has determined the Church: it is a *theologia semper reformanda* from various perspectives: the orientation laid down in the Gospel as normative, the mission of the Church, history, the signs of the times, the need for a translation of the message of the past into today's language and within today's horizon. To this extent there is no eternal timeless theology (*theologia perennis*). So theology must not only consider what has been decided by the Teaching Office but also think ahead; it must be *prospective*. It can then begin to ask new questions and make critical reflections from faith, for faith.

Pope John Paul II, in an important address during his 1980 visit to Altötting in Germany, spoke to theology professors concerning the position of theology in the Church:

> Theology is a science with all the possibilities of human perception. It is free in the application of methods and analyses. Nevertheless, theologians must see where they stand in relation to the faith of the Church. The credit for our faith goes not to ourselves; indeed it is "built upon the foundation of the Apostles and prophets, Jesus Christ himself being the chief cornerstone" (Eph 2:20). Theologians, too, must take faith as the basis. They can throw light on it and promote it, but they cannot produce it. They, too, have always stood on the shoulders of the fathers in the faith. They know that their specialized field

does not consist of purely historical objects in an artificial test-tube, but that it is a question of the faith of the Church as experienced in life.

The theologian therefore teaches not least in the name and on behalf of the religious community. He should and must make new proposals to contribute to the understanding of the faith, but they are only an offering to the whole Church. Much of what he says must be corrected and expanded in a fraternal dialogue until the Church as a whole can accept it. Theology is very much a selfless service for the community of the faithful. That is why objective disputation, fraternal dialogue, openness and the willingness to modify one's own views, are essential elements of it. . . .

Love for the concrete Church, which also includes belief in the testimony of faith and the *Magisterium* of the Church, does not estrange the theologian from his work and does not deprive that work of any of its indispensable self-reliance. The *Magisterium* and theology have two different tasks to perform. That is why neither can be reduced to the other. Yet they serve the one whole. But precisely on account of this configuration they must remain in consultation with one another. In the years since the Council you have furnished many examples of good co-operation between theology and the *Magisterium*. Let us deepen this basis. And whenever conflicts arise, apply your common efforts in the spirit of the common faith, of the same hope, and of the love that forms the bond between all of them.[38]

The Cologne Declaration was intended as an expression of this position.

Within this context we can refer to a 1981 resolution of the "Working Group of Catholic Dogmatic and Fundamental Theologians" on the relationship of the Teaching Office to theology. Even today its significance has not diminished. It is especially helpful today and contributes to a clarification of the issue.

> The Working Group of Catholic Dogmatic and Fundamental Theologians is convinced that Catholic theology as the science of faith is possible only in the community of the Church, on the foundation and within the norms of ecclesiastical faith.

---

38. *L'Osservatore Romano* (English edition), December 15, 1980, 17f.

Precisely because today it is a matter of making the Gospel, which the *magisterium* and theology must serve, present in credible and reasonable ways within the context of new questions and new cultures, bishops and theologians can fulfill their own responsibilities only in *loyal collaboration*.

Only in freedom can theology be of service in the Church and for the Church. Such freedom, founded on the Gospel itself, includes responsibility for unity and peace within the Church. But precisely for the sake of this service in the Church theology must be allowed both to explore freely and to discuss freely the results of this research. It must propose theses and hypotheses, the truth of which can be established only through discussion. It must make use of new methods and thus take into account the autonomy of the various specialized fields. In this way it can and must approach various schools and directions from the foundation of the one faith of the Church. One-sided theses and developments can be most effectively corrected by an unobstructed objective scholarly discussion.

Conflicts between the *magisterium* and individual theologians are always possible and even under some circumstances necessary for the sake of truth. Here both sides can overstep the boundaries. So it can be the right and duty of a theologian to admonish and criticize a representative of the *magisterium* if the latter speaks out in a theologically inappropriate way or improperly intrudes into the theological sphere. On the other side the Church's Teaching Office has the right and duty to call to account a theologian who, in the opinion of the *magisterium*, abandons or falsifies the fundaments of Catholic theology and thus causes confusion within the faith community. Such conflicts must be arbitrated by the two sides objectively and in a spirit of justice and brotherhood, without disparaging one another. Public polemics harm both sides and do not serve to build up the Church.

It is Catholic teaching that the final decisions in such conflicts are in the hands of the competent tribunals of the *magisterium*, if they are not expounded with final binding force, and can therefore be erroneous in principle but nevertheless claim proper respect. But because truth wishes to be convincing of itself, it can be expected that the *magisterium* will present such decisions with persuasive arguments and thus depend more on the power of truth and the force of the arguments than on administrative measures which dismiss open questions—

which behavior can severely damage the credibility of the
Church.[39]

But let us return to our theme.

In this context it is perhaps useful to consider the extent
to which criticism was directed against Peter in the New Testament, most sharply by Jesus himself (Matt 16:22) and then later
by Paul in the clash at Antioch where there was a question of
Jews and Gentiles sharing a table and Peter's conduct was im-
proper (Gal 2:11 ff.). Criticism of him and his conduct did not
harm Peter's special function but on the contrary drew attention to the significance of his being first among the Twelve and
to the extent to which his attitude characterized the community of believers. The explicit criticism of Peter in the New
Testament was constructive, not destructive. Why should we
not be able to concede the same appropriateness today to a
critique of the pope's conduct, of certain decisions and measures which are in no way infallible? Criticism of the pope has
existed throughout the history of the Church, most especially
in the Middle Ages. It was often expressed by saints—by
Bernard of Clairvaux and Catherine of Siena, to name only two.

During the Reformation papal criticism, especially by
Luther, went so far that he not only condemned individual acts
of the popes of his day, whose behavior was a detriment and
offense for the entire Church and bore no small blame for the
division within Christianity, but also repudiated the papacy
as an institution and ecclesiastical court of appeal, declaring
that the papacy was established in Rome by the devil and the
pope was the Antichrist predicted in the Bible.

The Cologne Declaration is far from such a mentality. Its
signatories affirm the papacy and its authoritative service for
the unity of the Church. Our questions refer merely to the way
and manner in which this service for unity is perceived con-

39. The text is found in W. Kern, ed., *Die Theologie und das Lehramt,*
Quaestiones disputatae (Freiburg: Herder, 1982) 91:234–237. Max Seckler
has contributed in a special way to the clarification of this question; see
Max Seckler, *Die schiefen Wände des Lehrhauses* (Freiburg: Herder, 1988),
especially 105–155; Max Seckler, in Heinrich Fries, ed., *Handbuch der Fundamentaltheologie* (Freiburg: Herder, 1988) 4:180–241.

cretely today. This is a legitimate question which cannot be considered solved simply by assertions and claims.

The Cologne Declaration reveals the distress in the Church and is an expression of a suffering from the Church for the sake of the Church and commitment to it and its credibility. It is interesting that the themes of the Cologne Declaration are the same as those taken up in this book, even though there had been no prior discussions. The themes simply emerged from the current situation and the praxis determining it. The Second Vatican Council and the afore-described discrepancy with the Church of the present served as the criterion for the Declaration.

If the signs of the times in general are a theological locus to be clarified in light of the Gospel, that is valid and true for the signs of the times within the Church itself. That is what we did. We did not make any "assumptions" in the process. Nor did we pass any overall judgments, but rather referred to the mentioned themes and to concrete facts which have aroused great distress and were and still are discussed in complete openness. So it is not unfair to carry this discussion into the public forum of the Church.

It is also incorrect to think that polarization arose in the Church because of the Cologne Declaration. This polarization had existed for a long time in the discrepancy between the Church of the Council and the Church of the present; it exists in the obvious discrepancy between the official Church teaching and the practice of the faithful (for example, in the question of birth control); it is there in existing groupings, however we may characterize them. The Cologne Declaration is also an instrument for a proper solution of the tensions persisting in the Church: not through disciplinary measures but through dialogue in the service of a common cause.

The bishops in general have remained silent about the recent measures and decisions from Rome although, thanks to the publicity so customary today, they could well have known that great unrest and anxiety as well as deep distress have arisen among the faithful precisely because of the praxis of naming bishops. Wherever one went recently, this theme was on the agenda, often with deep emotion. The recent great exodus from the Church is evidence of this. The number of those who still remain in the Church but distance themselves from it, who are part of a migration within, cannot even be estimated. In any case the Catholic Church has been damaged and has lost respect and credibility.

The Cologne Declaration was a clear plea for the rights and competence of the bishops. It is amazing that the response of the bishops' conference did not take up the issue at all, that it rejected the form, tone and style of the Declaration but remained silent on the substantive questions underlying them. The bishops sought to appease Rome and asked for acceptance of the relevant decisions.

John Henry Newman said that the *prophetic function of the Church* is the special duty of theologians. The tension between office and prophetic protest runs through the Bible as it does through Church history. Tensions therefore are not to be lamented; they are rather signs of life. Newman stated that theology ''has restrained and corrected such extravagances as have been committed . . . in the exercise of the regal and sacerdotal powers; nor is religion ever in greater danger than when . . . the Schools of theology have been broken up and ceased to be. . . . I say, then, Theology is the fundamental and regulating principle of the whole Church system.''[40]

It certainly cannot be said that every theology can claim to exercise a prophetic function. On the other hand, it is very true that there are theologians in whom the prophetic function is clearly visible, and theologians like John Henry Newman and Karl Rahner can be described in this way. Even in his lifetime Rahner experienced strong criticism, but it did not succeed in dissuading him from the prophetic task which he had undertaken out of faith and love for the Church and to which he felt himself obligated. It is characteristic of the Church that broad circles within the Catholic Church are working to bring the work and person of Karl Rahner into disrepute and to dismiss him as a transitory or disastrous phenomenon soon to be forgotten.

40. John Henry Newman, *The Via Media of the Anglican Church*, preface to the third edition (1877) (London: Longmans, Green and Co., 1918) I:xlvii.

An anonymous postcard sent to me read, ''Fries is always destructive of our holy Catholic Church. His friend Rahner, the amateur church builder, has already been brought to account. Lord, deliver us from these arrogant theologians. Woe to you, O scholars! Long live the Pope!'' My early death was hoped for so that the Church and the pope could be free of me.

It is not presumptuous to say that the Cologne Declaration falls into the category of the prophetic. The challenges it raises cannot be countered by saying that it can be considered a local experience, for our diagnosis of the situation is to be found in the Catholic Church throughout the world, nor by making accusations, but only by opening up a path of dialogue and communication on the basis of mutual trust. There are in fact constantly more signs that this has been taken into consideration. If that is the case much will have been accomplished and gained, and the Cologne Declaration will have achieved its goal.

We have seen the current sorrows from the Church in the notorious discrepancy between the Church in and during the Council and the Church of the present—within a period of something more than twenty years. Certainly the present situation of the Church is also determined to a great extent from outside, by the so-called spirit of the times, the *Zeitgeist*, by a growing secularism, by the various critiques of religion, by atrophy, by the evaporation of faith.

But the current condition of the Church is also essentially determined from within, evoked by the Church itself through the measures and decisions of its hierarchy, through the style and manner in which the Petrine office is perceived and presented today, through the deficient actualization of the meaning of *communio* and people of God as the basis of Church—through falling short of the hope, encouragement, and reliance on the Spirit which was the intention and goal of Vatican II. It is the falling away from what was once the concrete reality of the Catholic Church which brought the Church a large measure of assent, identification, and credibility, but which today has often been reversed.

11 What Is to Be Done?

First and foremost, remain in, do not abandon the Church and enter the inner emigration or you give up every possibility of being effective within the Church itself. Second, no throwing up your hands! Don't let yourself become embittered! Believe and know that today's Church too is an *ecclesia semper reformanda* and as a historically existing Church is always capable of starting over. Who would have thought that the elderly Pope John XXIII was capable of initiating the Church renewal realized in his Council? Anyone who leaves the Church because of the above events is dreadfully lacking in understanding of the Church. Such people confuse the Church with what they are battling against; they identify the Church with office and *curia* and its present praxis. They lack the faith which believes the *Church*.

Further: work on the renewal of the Church wherever you meet the concrete Church—in the local Church, in the congregation, which is not a sub-branch of the world Church but a local Church, Church as event. Here much is possible if one invests faith, courage, love and imagination. What happens locally has a ripple effect.

We should not make our sufferings from the Church our sole theme and then forget the gratifying dimensions. Even today there is joy from the Church, such as its indispensable mediation of Gospel and sacrament, the advocacy today by the Church for humans, for their value and rights, its commitment to peace, justice, and reconciliation, the raising of its voice for those who have no voice. Here a look at the Church in the third world, which is the hope of the Church of today and tomorrow, is a source of inspiration.

There is joy from the Church when one considers how many people in how many congregations continue to be committed or begin to commit themselves to this Church, who do not let themselves be bewildered, and who despite what Karl Rahner called a wintry-looking Church express their hope and certitude: Even in winter the seed is growing.

There is joy from the Church if one thinks of the many internal revolutions, activities and movements which have not rejected the Church but instead look forward and have become involved in a future full of promise.

Thus the present situation, the suffering from the Church, can also become a great opportunity and hope.